Now, We Want to Write!

Jan Turbill

Language Consultant
Metropolitan East Region, N.S.W. Department of Education

Distributed in the U.S.A.
by
HEINEMANN EDUCATIONAL BOOKS, INC.
70 Court Street
Portsmouth, New Hampshire 03801

PRIMARY ENGLISH TEACHING ASSOCIATION

Acknowledgments

I have been fortunate in being able to work closely with groups of teachers who have successfully met the challenge of mastering the new process-conference approach to teaching writing. Talking and working with them in their classrooms has been a great learning experience for me.

The expansion in 1982 of the St. George Writing Project from three to ten schools could not have happened without the steady support of Mr Eric Flood, Chairman of St. George Regional English Language Committee K-12, Mrs Noila Berglund, Studies/Services Inspector, and Mr Trevor Harrison, till recently Director of the St George Region. Their faith and foresight have been admirable not only because of the newness of the venture but also because they had to surmount difficulties created by restrictions and financial cuts.

My 'conference partner' Robyn Platt deserves special thanks. She has consistently brought fresh observations to my attention and has offered many useful comments on the first draft. Jacqui Coss's comments too have been appreciated.

My parents have put up with me through two Christmas vacations on the farm while I spent most of my days writing. I want to thank them deeply for looking after me, listening when I needed an audience, and bearing my frustrations when the writing wasn't going well.

The support and guiding pen of P.E.T.A.'s editor, Bob Walshe, has again been invaluable. I've learnt more about writing from Bob than in all my years at school and since and I can't thank him enough. He has contributed the final chapter, on the difficult subject of evaluation.

Typing has been graciously carried out by Julie Beasley and Val Fryer. Terry Jeff took the cover photo. And Bridge Printery has, as usual, been most helpful.

Finally, the children. They continually surprise and delight me with their enthusiasm. They stay fresh in these 'writing classrooms', which is one more testament to the genuineness of the process-conference approach. There's no better reward than to hear them say—'Now, we want to write!'

Cover design by Dorothy Dunphy

ISBN 0 909955 47 6

First published July 1983
Reprinted January 1984
Reprinted December 1984
© Primary English Teaching Association
P.O. Box 167, Rozelle, N.S.W. 2039 (02) 818 2591
Printed in Australia by
Bridge Printery Pty Ltd
29-35 Dunning Ave, Rosebery, N.S.W.

Contents

Another Book on Writing?

In March 1982 I held the first 'hot off the press' published copy of *No Better Way to Teach Writing* in my hands. It was finished. I found it hard to believe. A great deal of talking, thinking, listening, reading and writing had taken place — and now it was finished! At last it could be shared with readers.

Response to the book has been exciting and at times overwhelming. Four editions in less than a year. Strong interest in every Australian state. Hundreds of orders from New Zealand. Orders for over 1500 copies from the United States. And the orders keep coming.

But questions, comments and insights have kept coming too. So many that a sequel to *No Better Way* is clearly the only way to express the range of rich new possibilities that are emerging from classroom practice.

Especially I need to respond to the teachers in the original St. George Project who have said, 'We've learnt so much more this year which we can share with other teachers.' That Project has grown from 27 teachers in three schools to 70 in ten schools. They have been supported by three consultants, who also have much to share. And many other teachers from interstate have told me of their ideas and experiences.

So at the end of 1982, I find myself sitting down to sort through a host of written and oral comments, and to get them into shape in the only way I know — by writing 'another book on writing'.

What Children Say about the Approach

- 'Before we had this writing it was boring writing about the teacher's topic . . . Now, we want to write because we can write about anything we want . . .' *Matthew*, Yr 3.

- 'The best thing is that the teacher just doesn't put topics on the board, we don't have a time limit . . .' *Tracey-Anne*, Yr 3.

- 'When I am writing a new story I usually think for a day about what to write . . . Once I get started I take about a week to finish it . . . When I finish the first draft I conference with about four people then I write a perfect copy so it can be sent to a parent to be typed . . . When it is returned I do the cover and the pictures and then it's ready to be presented to the class . . .' *Sharon*, Yr 4.

- 'It is good having enough time to write, think and talk about your writing . . .' *Helen*, Yr 5.

- 'When I write a long story I get sick of it . . . So I leave it for a while and start another one . . . Then I might come back and finish the long one . . .' *Marie*, Yr 3.

- 'It makes you think hard and if you think hard enough you can come up with a real interesting story . . .' *Steve*, Yr 4.

- 'I enjoy writing this way because it makes my brain flow and makes my imagination go to work . . .' *Mohammed*, Yr 6.

- 'When you have finished your writing you feel proud of what you have learnt and done . . .' *Kiri*, Yr 6.

- 'I like it because we don't have to write about the same boring thing that everyone else is writing about . . . It's good because you don't have a set, non-speaking time to write a short story . . . I think it's more interesting writing mysteries, murders, true events and many others . . .' *Lisa*, Yr 6.

- 'I like reading my story to the whole class when it is finished . . .' *Vicki*, Yr 3.

- 'It's helping me a lot. Before I hated writing but now I enjoy it and I've learnt so much about writing . . .' *Fadi*, Yr 6.

- 'I love reading the books the other children write . . .' *Leah*, Yr 3.

- 'You have your story put in the school library and let the whole school read it . . . Isn't that great! . . .' *Michael*, Yr 3.

- 'I like writing this way because it enables me to write good stories over a length of time . . . I am able to choose my own topics and am given half an hour each day . . . My teacher is a great help when we get stuck and unable to find a suitable word . . . Before I tried this writing scheme, written expression was a dreaded hour, even though it was only once a week . . . Now I look forward to writing each day . . . Whoever came up with this way of doing writing in school came up with a great idea and I think it should be continued throughout the schools in NSW and Australia . . .' *Joe*, Yr 6.

What Teachers Say about the Approach

● 'I've never enjoyed teaching so much, nor got such great work from my kids so painlessly.' — *Dian Scott*

● 'Writing 1982-style is the best change made in my classroom this year. The first steps were slow and at times I wondered if I were achieving anything. It's surprising how set in their ways 11 year olds can become.' — *Joan Hoyle*

● 'The best thing about the process-conference approach is children want to write. They are proud of their writing and can see they are progressing. They are in charge, determining their own rate of learning and what they need to learn.' — *Denise Stuckey*

● 'In the beginning: be enthusiastic; be patient with yourself and the children; give them time to edit their work; keep on growing lists of topics; make sure all work is kept and dated by the children; read to them daily (all the time); encourage them to read each other's stories; don't expect great improvement during the first month; and remember, it's all worthwhile.' — *Cath Croucher*

What Principals Say

● 'Some teachers look upon the scheme at first as one that will run itself . . . They don't realise that it is harder than setting a topic once a week and collecting the books for marking . . . but as there are so many rewards it is worthwhile. We are finally individualising learning . . . So, my advice is: don't panic, take each lesson as it comes; don't lose hope, remember that others have been through the same; everyone has had some problems getting started; talk about what you are doing with other teachers and your principal; be prepared to change; accept that it is hard work and you'll get there.' — *Marilyn Kelly*, Oatley West Public School

● 'As Principal of a school which has been part of the St. George Project, I am thoroughly convinced there is "no better way to teach writing". I have seen the progress taking place in each class and seen each teacher working competently. However, I regret not actually having had the chance to teach the approach. My advice to colleagues is to find time to get into classrooms and work with your teachers.' — *Sister Margaret Harrison*, St. Aloysius Primary School

What a School Staff Says

● 'The conference approach succeeds in our school because:
- the whole school is involved;
- the teachers know they have support from each other, the executives and the consultants;
- we all believe in it, and the children enjoy it;
- we stuck to it (through thick and thin);
- we talk to one another about it;
- we are flexible and prepared to change;
- the children have learned to criticise constructively;
- the children are learning social skills;
- writing encompasses the entire curriculum.' — *Oatley West P.S.*

CHAPTER 1

Teaching the Writing Process

Teachers in their thousands world-wide have swung over to the 'conference approach' to teaching writing because they have realised that the old way — sometimes termed 'current-traditional' — is not producing either good writing or willing writers.

Why Change the Way You Teach Writing?

In essence the old way meant teacher-prescribed topics, little preparation for the writing, an expectation that writing should be completed at a single sitting, that the first draft should be the only one and should be 'correct', and that this draft should be handed in for marking by a teacher who would only have time to attend to its surface features, particularly its spelling, punctuation and grammar.

Teachers have decided to change to the new approach after hearing or reading evidence that childen do write willingly and can make relatively rapid progress when they are given more control of their writing and are helped more individually by the teacher, not just at the marking stage but by a series of 'conferences' at various stages of the writing 'process'.

Process? Conference? What do these terms mean in the context of the writing classroom?

The Writing Process

Writing is a process in the sense that it involves thinking, feeling, talking, reading — and writing. It is an extended effort to make a message clear. A 'one-shot' draft can seldom achieve this. A writer needs time and opportunity to think about what is to be written, to make decisions about the writing before, during and after drafting, and then to revise effectively so that the piece can be confidently presented to the intended reader with expectation of a positive response.

The following diagram assists discussion of writing as a process, but its author[1] warns that the 'stages' are never, in practice, a neat sequence of steps; rather, a writer moves to and fro through them — interactively or recursively — for example, by revising while drafting or drafting new material at the revision stage.

Experience or Problem	Pre-Writing	Draft Writing	Revising & Editing	Product & Publication	Readers' Response	Writer's Attitude
decision to write; growth of intention	incubating rehearsing discussing researching	inc. some revising while drafting	recasting polishing rewriting proofreading	appropriate format, despatched to readers	a response that is conveyed to the writer	feelings and reflections on this whole experience
PRE-WRITING		**WRITING**		**POST-WRITING**		

---

[1] R. D. Walshe, *Every Child Can Write!*, P.E.T.A., 1981, pp. 21, 29.

The Complex Process of Writing

Recently, at the Meanjin Writing Camp in Queensland, I asked 40 children, ages 10-13, what they think about while they are composing. Here is a summary of their responses . . .

Pre-writing	Writing/Revision	Post-writing
Feelings: anxiety, nervousness, sadness, fear, panic, criticism, confusion, hatred, blankness, humour, joy, anticipation.	*Write a draft*	*Give to a reader*
	Get the ideas down	*Perhaps try several readers*
Sense impressions: smells, sounds, pictures, fantasy pictures . . .	*Don't worry about spelling and punctuation yet*	*Seek advice, ideas, help*
Thinking, remembering	*Pen goes fast but mind goes faster*	*Illustrate, decide on cover*
Making decisions: where to start, how to plan, will I be too personal, should I be boastful, which questions in my head will I answer, who is the reader . . .	*Edit, shape, tighten, expand*	*Feel satisfied*
	Rewrite, thinking of audience and purpose	*Perhaps want to write again*
	Proofread	*What have I learned?*

N.B. The children's responses confirmed that there are no barriers between these stages; that writers move backwards and forwards, and that much depends on the *purpose of* and the *audience for* the piece of writing.

The Writing Conference

Extensive classroom research has tried to discover a workable way to individualise the teaching/learning of writing. From this has emerged an appreciation of 'the conference'. In its main form it is a brief discussion between teacher and child, and it may occur before, during and after the writing. Though in one sense it is simply a 'talk', it is also, for the teacher, an art of classroom management—chiefly the art of drawing forth ideas and fostering thinking, by asking questions. It encourages the young writer and stimulates him or her to improve the writing.

The Process-Conference Approach

The approach to writing outlined in *No Better Way to Teach Writing* has brought the ideas of 'process' and 'conference' together.[2] The conference is the chief means by which the teacher nurtures each child's process. A teacher who is sensitively aware of the writing process is able, through

---

[2] Two other books can be consulted on this approach: the P.E.T.A. publication, *Children Want to Write*, ed. R. D. Walshe (1981), and the Heinemann publication by the principal contributor to the approach, Donald H. Graves, *Writing: Teachers and Children at Work* (1983).

conferences, to assist a child when difficulties arise at any point in the process. Help is thus available where it is most effective — at the point of need. This is the great advantage of individualised *learning* over generalised *teaching*.

The approach can be viewed as resting on four pillars:

1. Time. Adequate daily time is provided for the children to practise properly the process of writing. They have time to think about, talk about and share their writing. They know for example that they can leave a piece of writing when it is not going well and start another piece or return to it at a later time.

2. Ownership. The control of and responsibility for the writing is left with the children. They choose topics to write about from their own experiences and interests. Unknown spellings are 'guessed' or 'invented' as the piece is written. Punctuation is often ignored in the early stages. The children establish the purpose and the audience for their writing and decide on an appropriate form and style. They decide whether to 'publish' the writing for others to read.

3. Process. There is an emphasis on the process of writing; to draft-revise-publish instead of merely writing a one-shot draft. Because daily time is set aside for writing, the young writer can be supported before and during the writing process as well as after the writing is finished.

4. Conference. These brief discussions with an individual child or small group of children may occur before, during and after the writing. During a conference with a child the teacher is providing support at his or her point of need, thus individualising the teaching/learning.

'It makes you think hard and if you think hard enough you can come up with a real interesting story,' says 9 year old Steve.

CHAPTER 2

Getting Started

'Initial chaos in this area is only a temporary state.'

Major change in human affairs is typically marked by some untidiness or disorder. Teachers should be prepared for a little 'chaos' when implementing the process-conference approach. But it won't last long.

The point is to *stop* the old way and give the new an enthusiastic *start*.

Successful classroom management is always a challenge. The Project teachers all needed to make many changes in class organisation both before and during implementation. Not all at once, of course, but as need arose. They continually assessed the situation, changing rules and strategies as they felt their way . . .

● *Chris Cookman:* 'It all became a matter of valuing and using your own judgment, initiative and commonsense.'

● *Francis Kean:* 'Discussion with other members of the staff helped iron out lots of problems.'

● *Shirley Stokes:* 'In the beginning, a lot of changes had to be made — for many, the changes were made slowly but surely . . . A major breakthrough occurred when the children assumed responsibility for their own writing.'

Jill Sweeting's Advice

'You need to plan several things. Here's how I started my Year 6 class:
- We discussed the approach and I suggested six months' trial;
- we planned a daily writing time suitable to the class and me;
- plenty of pens, pencils and paper were on hand;
- each child had a manilla folder to hold first drafts;
- I handed out 'Steps to Follow' (from p. 82 of *No Better Way* . . .);
- we discussed how these steps could be organised;
- I warned of a little chaos at first, but we'd learn together;
- I selected a writing partner for each child but after a few weeks they could choose their own partners;
- we discussed free choice of a writing topic.

AND SO WE BEGAN!'

● 'It helps the children in the beginning if you develop together a short list of topics. Finding their own topics at first, especially the older children, can be a little daunting.' — *Francis Kean*

Robyn Platt's Comprehensive Advice

[As part-time consultant to the St. George Writing Project, Robyn has very successfully helped many teachers K-6 to get started. — *J. T.*]

● **Collect** a variety of paper, lined, unlined and coloured; a variety of pens and pencils;

The list of topics on her writing folder reminds 8 year old Susan of what she has written about, and helps her to choose her next topic.

several large sheets of cardboard or newsprint and marker pens;
a number of favourite books from the library; and
your class, in the usual place for discussion sessions.

● **Begin** by discussing the books you have collected:
Who are the authors, illustrators, publishers?
What are the topics (titles)?
What are the possible reasons for choosing these?
Are the books factual, imaginative, descriptive, funny . . .?
(Emphasise that authors write about what is important to them —
things they want to share with readers through publication.)
How did they develop into this form? (Discuss drafting, revising,
working with an editor till the manuscript is ready for publishing.)

● **Announce** that everyone will be an author, including yourself;
every child will choose his or her own topics;
thinking-up, drafting, revising, and rewriting are legitimate uses of

the writing time by the child, while editing and typing for publication
will be carried out by the teacher (perhaps with a parent aide);
a daily time will be set aside for writing;
a piece of writing may take several days to complete.

● **Choose** a topic in the following way:
ask everyone to think of an interesting topic;
write your topic and theirs on a large sheet for all to see;
perhaps steer the children away from the usual 'school topics';
show the collection of writing paper, pens and pencils;
explain that first draft writing, with crossings-out and misspellings,
may not be tidy; it belongs to the author, who is its only reader at
this stage; ask everyone to *choose* from the listed topics or any other.

● **Write** on the chosen topics for ten minutes (teacher too);
be prepared for some interruptions during this first effort;
e.g. asked how to spell a word, say it doesn't matter at this stage;
any insecurity arising from this freedom will soon pass;
if you keep writing, they will feel encouraged to do so too.

● **Share** the writing after calling the class together:
advise that sharing at this unfinished stage is not compulsory, but
volunteers may exchange their drafts and discuss them;
read your own draft aloud to the class for discussion;
indicate ways you might later revise your draft.

● **End** this first writing session:
ask that the draft be dated and placed in a folder;
indicate what will happen tomorrow.

● **Subsequently**, day by day, clarify ideas such as: choosing one's
own topic and getting ideas before starting; first draft, revising,
rewriting and publishing; teacher and peer conferencing; value of
keeping one's own list of possible topics; and uses of the writing folder.

● **Construct** with the class a list of steps of the writing process that
need to precede acceptance of revised writing for publication —
and activities to go on with when the writing is finished.
This will help to keep the writing time hassle-free.

The central point is that the children will be writing daily and will be
learning to write through this writing.

Finally, here are some problems commonly encountered by teachers in
the early stages, especially with classes accustomed to a set topic, a fixed
time-limit and the handing in of first-draft writing:
• children not knowing what to write;
• an increase in the noise level;
• children's tendency to talk more about writing than to write;
• children not knowing how to edit their work;
• too many children clamouring for conferences;
• children who depend on teacher approval before moving on;
• apparent decline in quality of writing as quantity increases.
The teachers and the children learned to cope with these and other problems as their experience of the approach grew.

CHAPTER 3

Classroom Management

Remember, a classroom must be predictable . . .

Resources

The children need to know these are present:
- paper, pencils, rulers, sharpeners, stapler, etc.;
- dictionaries, atlases, class theme books, other reference books;
- various covers, into which writing is stapled or tied to make a book;
- the alphabet (especially for young children) displayed on a wall or pasted on the desk or inside each child's folder;
- display charts currently needed, e.g. 'Steps in the Writing Program' (see *No Better Way . . .*, p. 82), or 'Common Word Problems'.

Rules of Operation

The teachers found that classroom rules are best worked out in discussion with the children. Some found it useful to list the points on a chart and display this for a short period; thus, in Dorothy Jauncey's Year 4 class:

Ready for a Conference?

Have you read it to yourself aloud?
read it to your partner?
fixed up parts that don't make sense,
or don't have enough information?
fixed all the spelling and punctuation?

Children also need to know answers to questions such as these:
- What do I do if I can't think of a topic?
- What do I do if I can't spell a word?
- What do I do if I'm stuck or bored with my piece?
- What do I do if I need more information?
- What do I do if I need more paper?
- What do I do when I'm finished?

If the teacher and the children have answered these questions together there can be no excuse for children not getting on with their work. The responsibility lies with the child.

Storage

Children accumulate so many pieces of writing that they need to maintain an efficient storage system. Here are three systems used by Project teachers:

- Have two folders or large envelopes for each child: one for the writing drafts which, whether finished or unfinished, are not presently needed; the

Using the Writing Folder

Four sheets are prepared and pasted on the folder thus:

- *Front Cover:* 'Topics I Have Written About' (see below)
- *Inside Front Cover:* 'Topics I Could Write About'
- *Inside Back Cover:* 'Skills I Know in Writing'
- *Back Cover:* 'The Books I Have Read'

Example of Front Cover:

TOPICS I HAVE WRITTEN ABOUT

Begun	Title	Finished	Published	Type
15.2.83	Star Wars	18.2.83		Adventure fiction
21.2.83	A Day at Cricket			Report
22.2.83	The Great Race	25.2.83	x	Adventure narrative

. . . And so on. This becomes an instant check on the number of pieces finished and the number published. At the bottom of the page we also carry a list of 'Writing Types I Can Try' (e.g. Story, Novel, Play, Report, Book Review, Script for Radio or TV, Autobiography, Science Fiction, Jokes, Puns — see P.E.T.A.'s *PEN 9* for further ideas); this keeps a wide choice before the child. — *Denise Ryan*

other for the piece that is 'in progress'. The latter is kept under the child's desk, while the former is stored in an easily accessible position in the room.

- Use a ring-binder folder with sections such as: 'Writing in Progress', 'Unfinished Drafts', 'Completed Drafts', 'Published Drafts'. This system is particularly useful for older children.

- Use exercise books. Some children prefer to write in a book. Work can be dated and kept similarly to work done on paper.

Whatever system is used, be sure that *all* work is dated and kept, even jottings and notes. This work is the record of the child's progress. Some teachers decided after a term to keep only a sample of that term's work, others kept all the work of the year before selecting a sample.

The Teacher's Role

The teachers advise their colleagues to be:

- consistent but not inflexible
- prepared to change
- ready to listen more and talk less
- more observant of children's daily work
- *predictable* in the children's eyes.

The right combination of classroom and teacher predictability can create

The right combination of classroom and teacher predictability can create an environment—a 'writing community'—that is conducive to the development of young writers.

an environment — a 'writing community' — that is conducive to the development of these young writers.

Questioning Techniques

Children begin to anticipate the questions the teacher might ask. They learn to consider the response they might make. In time they solve such problems without needing the teacher's questions.

Donald Graves has suggested four 'questions that teach' or 'opening questions' which enable the teacher and child to discuss the latest piece of writing as succinctly as possible:

'How's the writing going?'
'What's the piece about?'
'What are you going to say next?'
'How can I help you?' (See 'Roving Conference', p. 22)

He argues that once children themselves learn to ask these questions they are able to identify some of their own problems and often solve them. Moreover they will ask the questions of one another.

Having asked a question the teacher must:

● *WAIT for an answer.* Wait up to 8-10 seconds, sometimes even more, if the child appears to be thinking. It is the child's responsibility to respond to the question. (Invariably teachers find waiting difficult, so they repeat the question, or ask another, or even provide an answer — which causes the child to learn that out-waiting the teacher saves thinking.)

• *LISTEN actively to the child's answer.* In this answer lies the clue to where the child is at and what the next teaching step might be . . . The child is teaching us what to teach next!

'I have learnt to ask better questions and wait for the child to answer. This has led to the child improving the writing.' — *Bob Spencer*

Expectations

Expect that the rules and strategies worked out with the class will be carried out; they are there to assist everyone to work well together. If they are not working, the situation needs to be assessed and a change made.

Likewise, criteria for achieving quality of work need to be established. For example, *expect the children will*:

• improve their writing over time;
• edit pieces they choose to publish;
• use the spelling and punctuation skills they know;
• attempt new modes (genres) of writing;
• see that edited work for publishing is clear and neat;
• learn to conference constructively with peers;
• learn to self-evaluate writing.

In short, expect them to make decisions and take increasing responsibility.

Using Time

Because children need to know how the writing time will be used, work out *with them* answers to these questions:

• What time of day do we write?
• For how long do we write?
• What activities are permitted, and not permitted, in writing time?
• If writing and reading times are integrated, will the integration provide enough time for each?

As a result of the discussion, a timetable can be drawn up together.

• 'How do we find time to write daily? The original recommendation of 5 half hour sessions was a good way to start. But for our class, in our school, this was not practical, so we varied it to 3 and sometimes 4 sessions of 45 minutes each. This variation suits us and has not led to any deterioration of their desire to write.' — *Bob Spencer* and *Prod Foulkare*

• 'I found it necessary to organise the half hour daily writing time in specific working units:

10 minutes: the children write quietly. (I move quickly around the class talking to those who appear stuck; then I write in the class record book things I have noted about the children from the day before or from the talks I have just had.)

10-15 minutes: the writing continues, with some children working in small groups, sharing their writing and asking questions of each other. (I work on a one-to-one basis with children who indicate they have a piece ready to be edited; I work with 4-6 children, often more.)

10 minutes: the children continue to work in small groups, sharing their writing and asking questions of each other. (I 'group conference': move around the groups, listening and asking questions.)

Variations to this time organisation include:

• Reading a story or part of one (sometimes a child's) at the beginning or end of the session to exemplify: good lead sentences, good vocabulary, good ending sentences, different styles, different modes.

• Writing by the whole class for a short time on a set topic.

• Discussion of problem areas with a third of the class at a time, e.g. using their conference time appropriately.

Time is at a premium during writing, so the class know we don't waste it.' — *Christine Green*

● Many teachers have found that a short period of 'Sustained Silent Writing' is useful. This can be writing on a set topic, or each child may choose a topic. All Barbara McNamara's Year 3 have a 'Three Minute Story Book'. A topic is selected each day and the class including the teacher write about it for three minutes. They spend another two minutes sharing a few pieces, discussing leads, how the story might develop and any interesting words that have been used. Rarely are these pieces finished in the three minutes, but the children may choose to finish the piece in the writing time.

Other teachers have found that children need an area or a signal which allows them to write without interruption. A 'No Talking' table where children can move to, or a large cardboard box with only three sides left, makes a good barrier to place on the writer's desk (re-covered old 'Breakthrough to Literacy Sentence Makers' make great barriers).

● Here are some other ways teachers use time:

(a) *KINDERGARTEN CLASS*

5 minutes: children on the mat as a class group and three or four in front, each with own 'published' book. (Teacher and child read book to class and show pictures.)

20 minutes: children work on writing in groups. (Teacher works with one group each day, talking about their pictures and writing.)

5 minutes: children clean up, move to mat, share their work. (Teacher selects children to share their work with class.)

(b) *YEAR 5 CLASS*

10 minutes: children begin work, writing, talking, reading. (Teacher conducts brief 'roving conferences'.)

15 minutes: group of 4-5 children come to the teacher, while others continue writing. (The group share work with each other and the teacher, discuss how to improve, and what to do next.)

10 minutes: individual children share their work, or parts of it, with the whole class. (Teacher points to 'specifics', e.g. lead sentences, punctuation, spelling, tightening of piece.)

(c) *YEAR 6 CLASS*

5 minutes: class discussion, e.g. of any problems or interesting sentences or thoughts. (Teacher helps in discussion or asks 'questions that teach':

Nine year old Melissa knows that, having revised and rewritten her piece, she must write her name in the Conference Book for a 'publishing conference'.

How are you going? What's it about? What will you say next? How can *we* help you?)

15 minutes: children carry on silent writing. (Teacher, at own table, works with individuals or a small group.)

10 minutes: children conference with each other. (Teacher moves around for 'roving conferences'; makes sure of seeing every child each week.)

● *IS THERE TIME TO CONFERENCE WITH ALL THE CHILDREN?*
To this key question, Denise Stuckey replies:

'Yes. Conferences only become too long and cumbersome because of the teacher. To justify to herself that she is teaching, she must spend a certain amount of time with each child in each lesson, and consequently some children always miss out. These are the children who don't demand attention *and* the children who need it!

'To change this situation, teachers must modify their concept of teaching: children do not need to be talked to (or at) for learning to take place. They need to be in an environment where they can learn. This environment must be *provided* by the teacher but it does not have to *revolve* around the teacher.

'Children learn through their own writing. In spelling they make their own modifications to their initial guesses (and *subsequent* guesses) so that a satisfactory result is gained. They do not need the assistance and approval of the teacher at each step. In many conference situations all that is required of the teacher is a sentence/statement concerning one particular area of the child's work so that the child can continue the work. But instead of providing this the teacher feels she must analyse and comment on all that the child has written. The teacher wants to feel needed and creates a situation in which she is.

'But if an environment is created where the children are free to make mistakes and decisions for themselves, then the amount of teacher time required by each individual child will decrease and the teacher will have the time to spend with those children who really do need her assistance.'

CHAPTER 4

The Conference

● 'Writing is thought-provoking, tiring, emotional and an insight into our own character. We teachers must be sensitive to the conditions under which the writing takes place.

'The conference is an excellent way of getting to know and understand each child. Questions such as, Why did you write that? or What makes you say this? delve into the reasoning and ideas behind what might have been a trivial tale. Helping the child to add those ideas turns the tale into an exciting piece. The conference is the key to better writing and better teaching.' — *Sue Hutchins*

The conference is the teaching, listening, responding, sharing, reacting, reflecting time of the writing sessions. In fact, it is the lynch-pin, and so the time spent on it is precious.

How Conferences Help

In the beginning many teachers find it difficult *not* to want to see every piece of writing the children do. And mostly the children expect their teachers to 'mark' everything they write; after all, that has been the usual practice. But after a while the children and the teachers accept that it is not necessary for all the writing to be read or marked.

But teachers do need to be aware of the child's interests and strengths and weaknesses and needs. This information can easily be obtained during brief conferences throughout the week and perhaps one major conference if it is necessary.

There are several types of conferences and they may range in time from a few seconds to ten or even fifteen minutes. Rarely should the teacher spend more than ten minutes with a child. If this is occurring, time is not being used expediently. A common problem is that the teacher could save time by leaving the child writing, moving to other children, and returning to the child in a few minutes. Another common problem is that the teacher does too much talking. Teachers must listen more and let the child talk.

Many teachers have found the need to label the various conferences, e.g. the roving conference, the sharing conference, the group conference, publications conference . . .

● 'At the core of the conference is a teacher asking a child to teach her about the subject. The aim is to foster a bursting desire to inform. So the teacher never implies a greater knowledge of this topic than the child possesses, nor treats the child as an inferior learner. We are in the business of helping children to value what they know. Ideally, the poorer the writing the greater interest the teacher will show in it — or rather in what it might become.' — *Donald H. Graves*

Roving Conference

The teacher moves or roves around the class, usually at the beginning of each writing session, *looking at*, not necessarily reading, the writing. Very quickly the teacher can: note how much writing has occurred since yesterday, check on children who were having problems, and identify children who are presently having problems. Opening questions might include:

How's it going?
What's the piece about?
What will you write next?
How can I help you?

● 'I find the roving conference very useful. It involves ten minutes at the beginning of each lesson. I wander around the room and see everyone's work. It gives me an idea of how everyone is going, the areas of difficulty and the children with problems. It saves me a lot of time to work with children who really need help.' — *Francis Kean*

● 'By using the roving conference I can see every child's piece of writing, note who is continuing a piece, who is starting a new piece, and actually work with about five children who may be having problems. This is how it works:

Teacher: This is a new story, Julie. What's it about?
Julie: About a kitten who goes to sea [starts writing] . . .
Teacher: How's it going, John?
John: I'm sick of it — I've written all this. [4 pages]
Teacher: What's it about?
John: About my cat, Garfield, and how I got him.
Teacher: Where have you written the part when you got him?
John: I've just written that now.
Teacher: What are these four pages about? Try writing me a list of the main points you are telling me, the reader, in those pages.

'Leaving John, I moved to three more children, checking where they were at and what they were going to write next, and I noted two more children who had almost finished. I suggested they get together for a sharing conference before putting their pieces into my tray — "for reading". (I would read them through, making notes for myself before asking them to join me in a publications conference at a later time; meanwhile they knew they were to start another piece.) I reached Ray on the other side of the room. He had been waiting for me. He had a problem:

Ray: I don't like the beginning of my story. It's all finished except for that. I've tried thinking of other leads but I can't think of anything else.
Teacher: Tell me what is happening in that first part?
Ray: I'm walking through an arcade — no — I'm wandering through an arcade looking at the sport shop — looking at the football boots. That's what it's about — the football boots are magic.
Teacher: Try turning that page over and starting again. Think of what you were doing or what you wanted . . .

Eight year old Darren, trying to find a way to start, describes his cracker night to his teacher.

Paul [waiting for me to finish with Ray]: I don't now what to write about.
Teacher: Why don't you read through Ray's and Lisa's topic list and then go and read some of the other children's published books? . . .

 'I returned to John . . .
John: I've written six things.
Teacher: Which bits of information does the reader need to know for your story about Garfield?
John [reading down his list]: Not that, nor that I guess.
Teacher: You think about it and discuss it with a friend . . .

 'I returned to Ray . . .
Ray: How does this sound? "Wandering through the arcade . . ." I think it's better.
Teacher: Yes, it sounds better than what you had . . .
Teacher: How's it going, Cheryl?
Cheryl: O.K. I'm just thinking what to write next.
Teacher: How can I help you?
Cheryl: You could read it and see if it makes sense so far. Lisa says it's O.K., but will you read it?
Teacher: Sure, put it in the Reading Tray.
Cheryl: I'll read it through again and then help Karen. Then I'll work on my poem . . .

'John was back into his piece about Garfield, having decided to leave out most of the first four pages.

'All that took me ten minutes. And then I was ready to work with children who were ready to publish a piece. I called the first child to my desk . . .'—*Jill Sweeting*, Year 6

Group Conference

There are many reasons for organising a group conference, including:

TO TEACH a point several children need, e.g. the use of 'speech marks' when direct speech is used.

TO INTRODUCE a different writing mode. For example, a group of children in a Year 5 class were experimenting with poetry. The teacher brought them together, gave them a pile of poetry anthologies and suggested they individually find a favourite to read to the group. After a few minutes the group were sharing poems and discussing the form each poem took. They moved away to write their own poetry but returned to the group situation to share their work, seeking ideas and better words. The group worked in this way for several days with little teacher assistance. At the end of the week they had a selection of poetry they wanted published.

TO SHARE their work. For example, when four or five children indicated they had finished a piece and would like to share it with others, they joined the teacher in a 'sharing group-conference'. Whilst this conference was in session the other children in the class knew they must not disturb the group. Each child in the group read the latest piece (or part of it if it was very long). The other members commented on the parts, words

The group conference can be used for teaching a point to several children or simply for sharing children's work.

or phrases they liked and also the parts, words or phrases that didn't make sense. The teacher's careful questioning led the writer to become aware of what needed to be done to the piece and also acted as a good model to the other members of the group. As the year proceeded, the children were better able to take over from the teacher and the discussion became group-oriented rather than teacher-oriented.

Whole Class Conference

There are times when it is useful to discuss an issue with the whole class. This type of conference is usually held at the beginning or end of a session and takes only a few minutes. It might involve the sharing of interesting lead sentences or words or phrases the children have written; or a discussion of general class rules of operation, or a demonstration of interesting uses of language by reading 'published' books, both commercial and child-authored.

Individual Conference

This conference should be short (as in the case of John and his problem with Garfield the Cat, above). But sometimes, when the child's first draft is finished and it is being prepared for publication, the conference may take ten minutes or so.

Remember, much of the work can be done by the child without the teacher actually sitting there all the time. Sometimes, however, a problem may occur which involves a great deal of discussion in order to sort out the meaning the child intends but hasn't written. When this happens, try to find time to work with the child during the lunch-break or at some other time in the day when the demand on teacher-time is not so heavy.

The writing time will involve all these types of conferences depending on the needs of the class.

● 'At first, the conference time was spent just listening to the children read their writing and then discussing it with them. But having worked on that individual level I soon noticed that there were group areas forming. This led to group lessons on things as they occurred. The writing was now totally shaping our language work. I found I was using the conference more and more as a teaching time and thus was individualising my teaching more and more. Then the children began to develop a conference style with each other, reading each other's work and suggesting ideas for improvement. The demand on my time was decreasing! I could spend more time with those children who really needed help. I believe I am now teaching every child at the level of his or her need. — *Wendy Stewart*

Peer Conference

Peer tutoring is a very useful teaching strategy. Children *can* conference with one another. In many classrooms there are set rules which prompt them to do so, requiring the child to have shared his or her work with another child before coming to the teacher. Thus at Oatley West Primary

'What do you think should come next?' asks 12 year old Alex of her writing partner.

School children are asked to:
> *Read It to the Wall*
> *Read It to Your Partner*
> *Read It to Me*

In the first of these steps the child reads aloud, listening for words left out, clumsy sentences and information not supplied. A conference partner has responsibility for making some comment supported with a reason. This requires the partner to be an active listener and not simply say, 'Yeah, it's good', because the writer is a friend.

Joan Hoyle comments: 'Where possible the reader of the child's piece joins me in the conference. This reader repeats the comments made to the writer. The writer discusses what changes were made, if any, as a result of the reader's comments. In this way both the reader and the writer are learning.'

Julie Flavell comments: 'A lot of time had to be spent in the beginning teaching the children how to conference with each other so they'd help with the meaning of the piece. They tended to help with the spelling and punctuation because that's what we'd demonstrated as being important through the old traditional methods of teaching writing.'

Jill Sweeting comments: 'I found it necessary to write up a child's story (with his permission) on an overhead transparency. As a class we conferenced that piece of writing. I emphasised the importance of making sure the message was clear. We did this at least once a week for a month.

Soon the children developed the art of looking for parts that were unclear and asking the appropriate questions. Now they concentrate on spelling and punctuation during the proofreading stage.'

Publishing Conference

Both teacher and child need to prepare for this conference so the time will be used fruitfully.

It's the child's responsibility to:
- have checked the piece, adding any missing information and correcting the spelling, punctuation and grammar as well as he or she can;
- have read it to a partner, listening to the partner's comments and making changes appropriately;
- have requested a conference with the teacher.

It's the teacher's responsibility to:
- have been aware of the child's piece of writing as it develops over a period;
- have read it through from time to time, particularly if it is a long piece, making comments where necessary;
- have read it again in preparation for the conference, making notes for discussion with the child;
- have noted the key teaching point in the piece to emphasise with the child.

Don't expect the child to correct everything. If however there are things in the writing that the teacher knows the child *can* correct, then return it to the child as being 'not yet ready for a publication conference'. The child is expected to edit and proofread as much as he or she can.

Points to Remember during the Conference

Play a low-key role, don't dominate or talk too much.
Show interest in what the child is trying to express.
Get to know the child's interests.
Be aware of the child's strengths and weaknesses in writing.
Leave the pencil in the child's hand.
Develop the art of questioning — so the child solves the problem.
Teach one skill at a time.
Be positive at all times.

'Now, how can I write this lead?' wonders 11 year old Ray.

CHAPTER 5

The Writing Time

Children chiefly 'learn to write by writing' but we should not underestimate the teacher's role in providing an environment conducive to such learning.

Writing in a 'Workshop' Environment

As previous chapters have shown . . .

This is an environment where the CHILDREN:
- write daily, each at his or her own pace and level;
- choose their own topic, style, mode (i.e. exercise 'ownership');
- feel confident in sharing first drafts with each other;
- respond constructively to each other's work;
- revise and polish with an eye to purpose and readers;
- publish in a form that is attractive to readers.

It is an environment where the TEACHER:
- is patient, caring, enthusiastic for the child's every effort;
- knows each child's strengths and weaknesses;
- helps the child with one or two skills at a time;
- encourages trial of new words, ideas, structures ('models');
- avoids inducing a fear of being 'marked wrong';
- challenges the child to set higher goals and expectations;
- provides real readers for the children to write for;
- confidently expects the child to improve as a writer.

Plainly, the teacher is not redundant while the children are 'learning to write by writing' in the conference classroom. The teacher still very much *teaches*, actively guiding the children to learn more about their writing. (And this role is the more warmly appreciated by children when their teacher sometimes writes with them.)

Some areas where active guidance is possible:

Pre-writing	Writing/Revision	Post-writing
1. Topic choice	5. Draft writing	15. Publishing:
2. Finding out	6. Revising and	for real readers;
3. Drawing	editing	arranging to
4. Research skills	7. Sequencing	publish;
	8. Good beginnings	response
	9. Good endings	(see p. 61)
	10. Expanding	
	11. Tightening	
	12. Proofreading	
	13. Punctuation	
	14. Spelling	

1. Topic Choice

● 'My Year 4 were thrilled when I said we were going to write every day on topics of their own choice. At first, some couldn't think of a topic, so we discussed possible ideas. It didn't take long to create a short list that suited everyone.' — *Francis Kean*

Children *can* find their own topics. When a child writes about things he or she has experienced — things that are really known and really cared about — then the responsibility or 'ownership' for the writing stays with the young writer, and a distinctive voice sounds through the writing. Teachers in the Project have all been thrilled and continually surprised by the diversity of the topics their pupils have chosen.

Each child keeps in the writing folder a growing list of 'Topics I Could Write On'. Here are some of the ideas currently being used by teachers to help the children extend and diversify their lists . . .

• Keep a Class Topic Book to which the children make additions whenever they hit on an interesting topic.
• Hold brainstorm sessions which list topics; then each child adds some of these to the personal list.
• Occasionally issue a sheet of 'The Latest in Topics for Writing', with items drawn from the two previous sources.
• Occasionally, set the whole class a topic arising from a shared experience, but encourage personal interpretation.
• Introduce the writing session by reading the class's latest published stories — they often suggest ideas to others.
• Suggest a survey of books in the library as a means of finding topics.
• Take the opening sentence(s) of a well-known book and invite children to write on from there.
• Collect pictures of all sorts (taped to cardboard) for a 'Topics' box; perhaps write a few questions on the back of each.
• Rewrite well-known stories or fairy tales, whether seriously, facetiously, as a send-up (parody), etc.
• After discussing the class's current grasp of story types, invite attempts at one of the types; e.g. younger pupils might settle for 'funny', 'spooky', 'space', 'factual', 'animals'; others widely discuss types/modes/genres.
• Offer models for emulation, e.g. books that have been enjoyed, such as 'Choose Your Own Adventure', or stories, poems, plays, comics.
• For further ideas, consult the comprehensive discussion of 'Topics for Writing' in *Every Child Can Write!*, by R. D. Walshe, PETA, pp. 59-120.

2. Finding Out

How do we help children (a) to find out that they need to know certain information in order to write effectively on a topic, (b) to think up, ask for, or seek out this information? We can show them the value of 'finding out' procedures . . .

• *Limit the topic*, a specific topic is easier than a general one.
• *Talk it over*, with a partner or small group, to get ideas.
• *Draw it*, because this usually helps to gather and clarify ideas.

Ten year olds, Gavin and Matthew, have talked over some ideas, and Matthew watches while Gavin jots them down.

- *Read about it*, as suggested for research in 4 below.
- *Brainstorm it*, by jotting down in any order what comes to mind.
- *Consider the reader*—it gives rise to ideas the reader will need.
- *Try out 'leads'*, a variety of openings always releases ideas.
- *Ask the 5Ws*, the journalist's Who? What? Where? When? Why?
- *Checklist of questions*, e.g. after reading a story, draw up a list of questions the author needed to answer (What is it about? Who are the main characters? Where is it set? etc.); this can then be displayed to guide the children's story-making. Older children, working in pairs or small groups, can quiz each other on their prospective individual topics. Each child lists the questions asked of him or her and thus has a guide to the finding-out that will be needed if the writing goes ahead. (The list can be a useful guide to the teacher when conferencing.) For example, for a story, *The King of the Brumbies*:

Questions	I know	Need more info.
What are brumbies?	✔	
Where do they live?	✔	
Who will be main character?	✔	
What danger do they face?		✔
What . . . etc.		✔

For the very young pupils, drawing is a means of finding and expressing ideas.

3. Drawing

For the very young pupils, drawing is a means of finding and expressing ideas. Even as they become competent in writing many will continue to use drawing as a way of sorting out their ideas before writing.

The teacher can guide the child to realise that a drawing needs to be clear if it is to express an intended message.

A willingness to revise writing can be cultivated by a teacher who asks a young child to tell the story of a drawing. By asking questions about parts that are unclear, the teacher leads the child to add information and sometimes delete unnecessary detail.

Such questioning, I have found, needs to bend at times to respect the special logic of the young. For instance, I asked 5 year old Mandy about her drawing of a big tree laden with oranges and a house in the corner of the page.

'It's about my mum picking oranges,' she explained.

'Where is your mum, then?'

'Oh, she's gone in the house to get a bucket.'

4. Research Skills

Traditionally the domain of reading, these skills are often left to librarians to teach. Not any more! Opportunities for teaching them arise frequently in writing sessions. For example . . .

Darren, age 6, began a writing session by searching the class library and bringing a large book to his desk: 'It's about dinosaurs. I can't remember the names of the biggest one or the one that flied. It's in this book, you know.'

Christopher, age 8, having finished a first draft on turtles and finding his friend critical of it, asked his teacher for a book on the subject. The teacher sent him to the school library. He spent two sessions reading about turtles and revising his piece. Published as 'The Interesting Turtles' it is now a factual resource in the class library.

Karen, age 11, wanted to write 'not a report but a story, like Blinky Bill, about wombats — for little kids'. She listed questions about what they eat, where they live, etc., then spent a week with library books, making extensive notes. When the story was finished it had seven chapters. It was delivered with a flourish to Year 3 children, who prize it.

5. Drafting

● 'My class, having been used to writing once a week on a set topic and handing it in to me for marking, found it hard to change to writing a draft. They still tended to concentrate on neatness, correct spelling and punctuation at the expense of getting the information onto the page. I found writing a "draft" on the chalkboard an effective method of demonstrating the notion of draft writing. Once they saw me concentrating less on neatness, spelling and punctuation and more on getting the message down, they too began to free up in their writing.' — *Shirley Stokes*

Children need to be taught how to 'splurge' in their drafting and to leave most of the revising and proofreading until later in the process. They need to understand that the draft is for sorting out ideas and getting them down on the page. If they are pleased with what is written, they can then decide to revise and polish the piece, with an eye to the purpose and the readers of the writing.

● Ten year old Glen had just completed the draft of a letter to the Japanese Government condemning the slaughter of the dolphins. 'I didn't start out to write a letter', he explained as he showed it to me. 'We'd been talking in Social Studies about the slaughter of animals by man and I decided to write about the killing of all those dolphins. I was really mad! When I finished, I thought I could send it to the Japanese Government. So I wrote the story like a letter. If everyone did that they might stop, do you think?' He wrote two more drafts before he was satisfied. Then he handwrote the letter and sent it to Japan.

Once children begin to understand the notion of *the draft*, another problem can crop up; namely, convincing them they should date and keep *all* their drafts. They develop an adult urge to throw away drafts they no longer feel are needed.

• 'The first reaction of my Year 5 class was to throw away drafts they didn't feel they needed. Their folders were empty! They needed convincing that those drafts were necessary. I took a couple of kids' folders (with drafts) and demonstrated firstly that the drafts were a record for me and their parents to show they had been writing and not goofing around. Secondly, I showed them the progress we could see these kids had made over time. Thirdly, we discussed how these pieces were always there if the owners ever wanted to finish one, or take a piece out of another, or simply copy a word or an idea out of a piece. Now they understand why we keep our drafts, so they carefully date each piece, stapling together the notes and drafts done for a topic.'—*Tom McCabe*

6. Revising

• 'Writing only truly becomes writing in revision. A professional's first draft is often not much better than anyone else's. It is chiefly in revision that the professional's experience and draftsmanship show.'—Donald H. Graves, in *Children Want to Write*, ed. R. D. Walshe (P.E.T.A.), p. 13.

We have to show children that nearly everyone's first draft is rather unsatisfactory. The basic ideas may be there, but the piece will only become satisfactory for readers through careful *revision*; that is, when the

Eight year old Lisa needs to say her words aloud as she writes her draft.

'That part doesn't make sense,' explains 9 year old Julie as she helps Ian to revise his piece.

writer adds, deletes, changes or rearranges words and parts of the writing, and corrects omissions and slips in spelling and punctuation. By such a process the writing which earlier was a lump of clay has been shaped and moulded into a work of art. It is ready to be viewed by others.

As children grow older they become more willing to revise because they become more aware of the critical audience who will read their writing. For younger children, simply adding a word or changing a phrase may be the extent of the revision. They should be encouraged to revise as much as they can but not be forced to do so or they may stop writing. As 10 year old David explained, 'If I write long stories I then have to spend ages fixing them up and that's boring. So I just write short ones.' Too much had been expected from David and he (justifiably?) had made a compromise. But with careful coaxing from his teacher and the pressure of his peers, his stories are now growing in quantity and, with a little more revision each time, in quality.

Young children need help with 'how-to-revise strategies'. As 7 year old Sara explains: 'I can't write any more about the calf because I can't fit it in there', pointing to the lines of writing filling the page. 'You just can't move those lines of words up and those lines of words down, you know.'

Of course, Sara is right. But she can be shown some of the editing strategies that writers use. These strategies are not part of the print that

Sara has seen around her. She is used to seeing print set out neatly and correctly, so it is not surprising that she has expected her writing to be the same.

As with draft writing, teachers find that editing strategies can be easily demonstrated on the chalkboard as the need arises, whether to the whole class or to an individual child in conference.

Wendy Stewart found working with her whole class useful. 'Once a week my class and I write a story together. One child will write on the chalkboard while the others help with what to say, its sequence, and how to say it. We don't use the chalkboard duster. Rather we cross out, use the inverted "v", and draw arrows all over the place. The story looks a mess when we've finished. But it is clear. It's how we want it to go. We then check the spelling and punctuation. Finally, I copy it down neatly in our Class Story Book. As a result of such demonstrations the children are now able to adopt editing strategies quite easily in their own writing. This same activity can be used to emphasise story beginnings, interesting sentence beginnings, sequencing, story endings, interesting vocabulary and the elimination of too many *ands* and *and thens*.'

Most of the skills of revising can be taught individually in conference (see the previous chapter) but there are also group or whole class occasions when the teacher can show children 'how to make your writing better'. Not surprisingly these can become occasions for reading and language activities too. *Items 7-11 below present revision ideas collected from Project teachers.*

7. Sequencing

In speech we may be able to ramble or backtrack or repeat ourselves without giving offence — but not in writing! Writing demands an orderly ('logical') sequence of ideas. Some children, finding this difficult to achieve, need help in arranging their sentences.

Time Lines. To help young children, construct simple time lines. For example, What do we do at 9.00 a.m., 10.00 a.m., etc.? (It can be integrated with Maths.) Or draw one up after reading a popular story to the class.

Cartoon Strips. Simple cartoon strips such as 'Charlie Brown' or 'B.C.' can be backed with cardboard, cut into individual squares, and each set secured with an elastic band. A child or pair or group can decide on the best sequence. (For variation, erase the words and let the children write the script.)

Poems. Copy known or simple unknown poems onto cards. Cut into lines or pairs of lines. The children then read and sequence them. Group discussion of reasons for sequencing is valuable.

Short Stories. Similar to the poems, cut a story into sections for sequencing. Group discussion of reasons should follow.

The Children's Own Stories. Working in pairs, each child cuts up his or her own story into sections which the other then arranges. Both discuss their justification of differences — especially valuable for helping an author realise there were 'gaps' in the exposition.

'What's the best way to start this?' thinks 9 year old Gary.

Tina, age 8, had written about her snow holiday. Its sequence, from starting out to 'then we were home', was strictly chronological. When her partner sequenced it differently, highlighting 'good bits', Tina declared, 'There's only one way the bits can go.' 'Not for me,' said the partner. 'It doesn't matter what order some of these go.' Tina saw the point, rewrote, and this time began with the car trip home, taking the reader through the 'good bits', interspersed with references to events of the home journey such as, 'We'll stop for petrol here and get an iceblock.'

8. Good Beginnings

The question the child must ask of a beginning is: Does this lead 'grab' the interest of the reader?

Discuss the 'Good Lead'. Read some opening sentences or paragraphs of books recently read by the class. Ask, 'Is this a good lead?' or 'What confused you at first? Could it have been better? How?'

Share Professional Writers' Leads. Ask the children to find and share leads that have 'grabbed' or 'hooked' them. What information has the author of each lead conveyed? Using these models, the children can write, collectively or individually, the lead for a suggested story or two. Older children can also compare story leads with those used typically by news reports and non-fiction books.

Share the Children's Leads. In small groups or pairs, the children share the lead from their latest writing. Each then rewrites his or her lead on a new sheet. They share these and then rewrite a third lead. Which is best? The author decides after listening to opinions . . . Having 'played' in this way several times, the children are asked to use this strategy when revising. There is often some avoidance of doing so, but they soon learn that the second or third lead is usually the one chosen for the final draft.

● *Simon*, age 11, had written: 'It was another hot dry day in December 1982. The animals in the bush were about to experience a catastrophe. A long way off, in the bush, a small fire began around an old beer bottle carelessly left behind by picknickers . . .'

Only after much protest did he write another lead:

'The hot dry air began to move. Parched brown grass rustled and the branches of the tall eucalypts began to sway. The lazy old wombat sniffed — no rain coming yet. The majestic red kangaroo stopped grazing and lifted his head slowly towards the increasing breeze. His muscles tightened. He sensed danger. Smoke, he could smell smoke; a long way off yet, but it was warning of what might come. A long way off in the bush . . .'

Simon was thrilled with his second lead: 'I didn't think I could write a better lead — but I did!'

● *Jodi*, age 10, read her lead to Rodina: 'One day when I was walking home from school I discovered I was lifting from the ground . . .' 'What part do you remember?' she asked. Rodina replied, 'You lifting from the ground.' 'Thanks,' said Jodi and began to cross out. Then she rewrote: 'What on earth is happening to me? I seem to be lifting off the ground? . . .' Jodi had overcome the 'One day . . .' opening!

9. Good Endings

The question a child must ask of an ending is: Does this ending round off my story gracefully or is it too abrupt or flat?

Models from Literature. Discuss the endings of books and stories recently read by the class. Show the variety; for instance, some are predictable, others surprising, and a few leave the reader guessing. (The 'Choose Your Own Adventure' stories show a variety.) If the children rewrite in their own way the endings of several stories that are well-known to them, they appreciate better why the authors ended as they did.

Focus on the Children's Endings. Over a period, collect stereotyped endings currently being used by the children. List them for discussion: '. . . and then we went home.', 'I woke up and found it had been a dream.', '. . . they lived happily ever after.', etc. The children, in pairs, can attempt more satisfactory endings.

Knowing When to End. A major problem for some children is not knowing when to end. What should have been a short interesting story

'Why did you end it that way?' asks 12 year old Michelle of Peter.

rambles on and on. One teacher asks such children to draw each of the events in the story. They find this boring as they keep repeating a great deal in many of the drawings. In discussion they realise that they can rewrite the piece using only the events in the interesting drawings. Tighter writing results.

10. Expanding

Questions the child needs to ask of the first draft are: What further information will the reader need? What words will make the story more interesting?

Expanding General Statements. Children often write statements such as 'It was fantastic' or 'It was sad', which conceal information needed by the reader.

● *Peter*, age 8, had written 'Cracker Night', about the crackers he had and the building and lighting of the bonfire. When he came to letting off the crackers he simply wrote: 'It was fantastic!' In discussion he told me of noises, colours, the relighting of unexploded crackers and—lots more. I asked him to take another piece of paper and write all those thoughts down *specifically*, just as they came into his head. He did so then returned to his draft to add an exciting paragraph in place of 'It was fantastic'.

Asking a Reader. The most obvious way to discover whether information needs to be added to a draft is to try reading it to someone — to a writing partner, a small group, or a whole class.

● *Karen*, age 11, took her draft of 'The Stars in the Sky' to a Year 3 class. She read a portion at a time, stopping to ask for comments. Had the children been helpful? 'Oh yes,' she replied. 'I didn't realise that so many parts were confusing. I need to explain more about why the wombats went on their trek, and lots of other little things need to be added. I didn't think they'd be so clever.'

Completely Rewriting. Rewrite the whole story without referring to the first draft? Not many writers either want to or consider that they need to, but 10 year old Brett, who is shaping as a good writer, recommends it as a splendid revising strategy.

● *Brett* says: 'I write my first draft and then I read it through. I add a few words here and there. Then I ask my friend to read it and tell me the bits that are boring or he doesn't understand. I explain to him what I meant to write then I take another piece of paper and write the story again. This time I add all the bits that are missing. I do that sometimes up to five times until it is ready. If I don't like the story I stop and don't finish it. This is my latest story and I wrote that five times. Now it is ready.' And he adds, 'I tell my friends if they don't want to write the whole thing out again just to write a piece of it.'

Comparison of Brett's drafts reveals interesting expansions:
'The robbers dodged down the freeway.'
'The robbers dodged down the freeway causing great disruption.'
'The robbers dodged down the highway causing great disruption by running innocent drivers off the road and into other vehicles.'

'The car stopped at the wharf and boarded a boat.'
'The car stopped at the wharf and boarded a boat and sped off.'
'The car stopped at the wharf boarded a boat and took off away from danger.'
'The car stopped at the wharf. The robbers jumped out and boarding a boat sped off out of danger.'
'The getaway car screeched to a stop at the edge of the wharf. The Dwarf Gang jumped out and boarding a waiting boat sped off out of danger.'

11. Tightening

A question the child needs to ask of the first draft is: What words, phrases or information are unnecessary for the reader?

Use Literature as a Model. It demonstrates that good authors are economical with words.

● *Judy Wagner* says: 'I never realised what a great resource literature can be for the teaching of writing. Now I use it for everything. Every now and then I write a complex sentence on the board from a book we have just read. We discuss how many ideas are in the sentence and try writing it in as many small sentences as we can. We then examine the words the author used to connect all these sentences together. Sometimes we try to connect them in different ways. I call this game "Challenge the Author". I also use examples from the children's writing (with their permission). Together we work on the piece, tightening it into more cohesive writing. This activity is far more useful than isolated exercises out of a textbook.'

Prune Like a Gardener. Ask the young writers to become gardeners: 'Prune or trim all the unnecessary and untidy parts of the bush.' This 'game' should first be demonstrated to the class, then individuals or writing partners can practise it.

● *Pedro*, age 10, read his draft to a partner: 'My name is Pedro. I am ten years old. I want to introduce you to my pet cat. His name is Tiger. He looks like a tiger. He has black stripes and orange stripes on this back, and grey and white fur on his tummy.' They carefully pruned, polished *and expanded*, yet the improved version had fewer words than the first: 'Hi, my name is Pedro. Let me introduce my pet kitten. He has orange and black stripes on his back, and grey and white fur on his tummy, so we call him Tiger. He really acts like a Tiger too.'

Tighten by Limiting the Topic. Sometimes topics are so wide that the writing can only be general — or rambling. The topic needs to be limited or broken into several specific topics.

● *Tim*, age 8, wrote five pages about 'The Sea', attempting to treat, in some depth, sharks, spearfishing, sailing, water-skiing and more. 'What do you think is the best part?' his teacher asked. 'The sharks. I know a lot about them,' he replied. Tim eventually published a book on 'Sharks', full of specific information. It has become popular with his classmates.

These 8 years olds help eliminate unnecessary parts in John's piece by 'pruning like gardeners'.

12. Proofreading

At last the story is clear. It has been thoroughly revised. It can be rewritten neatly in a 'fair copy', ready for publication. But when the rewriting is finished, a final *proofreading* must be carried out. This is the checking of 'surface features', particularly spelling and punctuation. They are important because readers need to be able to focus on the writer's meaning without being distracted by errors or omissions.

Naturally young children won't be able to correct all their spelling 'inventions' and their slips, nor insert all necessary punctuation. But we *can* expect them to 'fix' what we know they can do. This will vary from child to child and grade to grade. They can be helped by the opinion of writing partners. Finally, what a writer and partner cannot do, the teacher as 'publications editor' will do for them in the interests of delivering correct — 'edited' — writing to the intended readers.

A great deal of spelling and punctuation will be learned during the writing time, and there will be further learning from the edited published version. From these *writing* sources, children will become observant of the spelling and punctuation in their *reading*.

13. Punctuation

Punctuation is for the reader; its 'points' are signposts which assist the reader to find his or her way through the words on the page. To punctuate well, the writer needs a strong awareness of the intended reader. Some suggestions:
- For young children, take every opportunity in their reading and writing to point out punctuation to them.
- The 'shared-book experience', using commercial 'big books' or class-made ones, offers opportunities to teach punctuation.
- Put short, unpunctuated passages of the children's writing on the board (with their permission) so the class can collectively punctuate them.
- Encourage reference to books in the class library when children are unsure about punctuating (e.g. for dialogue).
- Encourage the reading of writing aloud to listen for pauses where punctuation points may be needed.
- Discuss how writers use punctuation for various effects. (See *Every Child Can Write!*, by R. D. Walshe, P.E.T.A., 1981, p. 241.)

14. Spelling

Learning to spell needs to be closely integrated with learning to write. Much recent research shows that spelling can largely be learned as part of carrying out the process of writing (See P.E.T.A.'s *P.E.N. 36*, 'Teaching Spelling in the New Context'). Of course, reading too is a source of learning to spell. The child's writing and reading are interweaving day by day; but whereas reading brings innumerable *impressions* of spelling to the brain, it is writing for readers that impels the learner to clarify these impressions and get the spelling correct.

Nine year olds, Michael and Greg, know that the best time to concentrate on the checking of their spelling is at the revision stage of writing.

Every writing time can be seen as, incidentally, a spelling workshop. The child is learning to spell while writing, and this calls especially for developing a self-correction habit. There is little need — and some teachers believe no need — for spelling lessons that are separate from the writing time. Certainly there is no need for drilling of commercial spelling lists. And if a weekly spelling list is considered useful, then it is put together from words the child has currently misspelled and words the teacher knows will be needed in coming work.

Spelling in the New Context. The teacher conveys to the child a 'process view' of learning to spell while writing: 'Don't stop to ponder a spelling at the drafting stage, just write an invented spelling of the word and flow on with the composing of meaning; but return at the revision stage to check the spelling, and if you still have a doubt, settle it at the final-writing-and-proofreading stage by asking someone or by consulting a dictionary.' (*P.E.N. 36*)

More specifically the teacher will promote SELF-CORRECTION thus:

- *At the Prewriting Stage:* 'Watch for new spelling, especially when copying research notes from books.'
- *At the First Draft Stage:* 'Spell the word as best you can and flow on; or mark it so you can return to it later.'
- *At the Revision Stage:* 'Return to any doubtful word. Try out several versions on paper till one satisfies you. If still unsure, ask someone or con-

sult a dictionary. (Record the word in your personal spelling list for later revision.)'

- *At the Publication Stage:* 'Be scrupulous about proofreading. Solve any final doubt by asking your teacher.'

• **Note on Invented Spelling.** This subject has been treated at length in *No Better Way to Teach Writing*, ed. Jan Turbill, P.E.T.A., 1981. Donald H. Graves has devoted a chapter to it, and many other references, in his *Writing: Teachers and Children at Work*, Heinemann, 1983. For a comprehensive text, see Glenda L. Bissex's *Gnys at Work*, Harvard University Press, 1980.

Following are spelling experiences reported by Project teachers . . .

Don't Stop the Flow! How can we encourage children to concentrate on getting the meaning clear at the draft stage and *not* stop to ask 'How do you spell . . .'? Barbara McNamara called together her Year 3 children who were thus stopping. 'I suggested a compromise which, after discussion, they happily accepted. They would write part of the word and leave the rest blank for me to fill in. Now, after several weeks, only one child sticks to this. The others have all forgotten and write on merrily, guessing the words they need but can't spell.'

Teach Spelling in Conference. Robyn Platt says that generally, she picks one or two words the child has *almost* spelt correctly or has spelt in several ways. She proceeds to help the child . . . 'Simon, what is that word?' She points to *cot* in his sentence, *The whale cot loost.* 'Got,' says Simon. She writes *cot* on her piece of paper. 'What does that say now?' He sounds it quietly and says, '*Cot*, but it's supposed to say *got*.' Taking a pencil he changes the *c* to *g* in his piece. 'There, now it's right.' 'Good, now write on my paper all the ways you've written *watch*.' He lists *wat, wact, wath, watct*. 'Which is the closest spelling, Simon?' He points to *watct*. 'Which part is wrong?' He points to the *ct*. 'What sound is on the end?' '*Ch*,' he replies confidently, 'but I don't know how to write *ch*.' 'It's in *children*, on our board,' she says, 'so close your eyes and try to see the beginning of *children*.' With eyes tightly closed he feels for the paper and writes *ch*; then, opening his eyes, writes it again. 'There,' he says with a grin, 'that's *ch*! Now I'll write *watch*.' And he does.

A Self-correction Procedure. Ask children to circle five or six words they know they have misspelt or invented and would like to learn. On a separate sheet they write each of the words in as many ways as they think it might be spelt, then underline the one they believe is correct. Next, they consult a resource for verification — reference books, a dictionary, another child, or the teacher. When the list is correct the children write the words into their stories and personal dictionaries. If further memorisation of the words is needed the children can follow the Look-Cover-Write-Check 'study method'.

Make Use of the 'Study Method'. Devised by Ernest Horn in 1919, it has stood the test of time. Its essentials:
Look   at the word and say it to yourself;
Cover   it, close your eyes, and 'see' it;
Write   out the spelling;
Check   it, and if incorrect, repeat the steps.

Select Own Lists. In replacing the widely discredited textbook spelling lists, teachers are increasingly requiring children to select, or help to select, words for more meaningful spelling lists. Many classroom experiments on the how-to of doing this are proceeding. Common to all are words drawn from the child's personal writing. To these may be added: words drawn by the child from current reading; words drawn by the teacher from current work in all subject areas; words useful for illustrating roots, suffixes, prefixes, compounds and other features of word exploration; and words which lend themselves to 'word play'.

Various games can be played to help children learn their list words, without involving the teacher in marking. Two examples:
Write Your Own Dictation. Each child writes a passage (or sentences), using as many words as possible from this week's list (and perhaps previous lists). Partners first check the passage and then each gives it as 'dictation' to the other. Together they then check for correctness, with a dictionary to hand. The teacher sometimes checks as a safeguard against carelessness.
Challenge Me! Each child puts a mark on list words she or he claims to know how to spell. A challenger reads them out while the child spells orally. Any misspellings are noted and the child has to learn them by using Look-Cover-Write-Check.

A Weekly Contract. Marilyn Kelly, Principal of Oatley West, tells how the school has changed from 'the futile whole-class spelling list' to a weekly 'contract' which every teacher can flexibly adapt. First, each child chooses a certain number of words on Friday, including words from the week's writing, troublesome words, and words from the various subject areas; this list is written in the child's Spelling Book and it is checked by the teacher. Second, the teacher presents the weekly Contract, which tells what is expected in each spelling period of the coming week. It contains a strong element of word play. The child applies it to his or her individual list and this work is monitored by the teacher on the Friday while the children are drawing up their next lists.

Spelling Games and Activities. Oatley West's and other schools' games and activities are varied. They might include:

Listing words alphabetically	constructing word banks
word-building, word families	making crosswords
using words in sentences	word-making from letter groups
listing name (noun) words	noting words with silent letters
changing parts of speech	jumbling letters for deciphering
identifying syllables	tracing word origins
using prefixes, suffixes	learning root meanings

Many teachers (and perhaps the experts too) are in some doubt as to whether these are really *spelling* activities. Or are they 'vocabulary' or

Ellen and Bjorn consult a dictionary while proofreading their story prior to its publication.

'language' or just 'fun' activities? Which reminds us that some teachers reject separate spelling periods and believe that all spelling is best learned within the writing time, with emphasis on self-correction procedures.

Partner Problem. Francis Kean found that some children were crossing out a partner's *correct* spellings — in a misguided bid to find as many errors as possible! A solution was devised: the child who owns the writing holds the pencil when the partners go through a piece, underlining words they agree are wrong and putting a question mark over words in doubt. They consult a dictionary when necessary and only the author writes in the corrections.

15. Publishing

'The essence of publication is not just producing a "book"; it is getting the writing to readers — getting it read. Writers need to think hard about their intended readers, about what will interest them, and about a *form of publication that will attract them.*' (*No Better Way to Teach Writing*, ed. Jan Turbill, P.E.T.A., 1982, p. 61.)

Indeed, getting the writing to readers in a form that will attract them is a challenge to both teacher and child. The most popular form of publication has been 'the book'. Classroom libraries are filled with child authored and illustrated books which often become the most widely read books in the room. School libraries reserve a special place for the best of these books so they can be borrowed and read by children throughout the school.

How to Get Writing 'Published'? In the commercial world, it would be unthinkable for an author to 'handwrite' his or her manuscript. It is printed by a printery for a publisher. How can schools emulate this? Many are trying — using the typewriter and, when multiple copies are needed, the copying machine. But careful organisation is indispensable.

Dot Gamble works hard at publishing her Year 1 children's writing: 'Although I never correct the writing in front of the child I have no trouble deciphering the "invented spelling" as I've always had a conference with that child. I have to take the writing home to publish it. I write it into large books which are housed in the class library. As well, I make small booklets (6cm x 8cm) with cardboard covers. I write the story into these with the title and author on the cover, and the children take great delight in illustrating them. Each has a folder, similar to a "Breakthrough to Literacy Folder", with cardboard slits inside, into which the small books can be slid. By the end of the year each child will have a folder of "Little Books" to present to his or her parents. Until then they are displayed prominently in the room and are a source of great interest to all who visit us — and of course great pride to their owners.'

Sue Hewitt confirms that when the teacher tries to do all the publishing herself, pressure becomes heavy: 'It can be a real nuisance at times, especially with Kindergarten. They want their writing published NOW. I used the large-print typewriter and at first could easily do two or three each morning, using large sheets of art paper. I typed the sentence(s) on the top of the page and inserted this into a cover made from wallpaper

The children's published books need to be prominently displayed as part of the class library.

sample books. The children would then draw another picture or cut up the original and paste it in. When the book was completed I would "read" it to the class, sometimes pointing out things like fullstops, spaces between words and where in the room a particular word could be found. But now, towards the end of the year, the children are writing so much that I can't possibly publish as many stories. So I have been forced to tighten the publishing criteria. We share as much writing as we can but only select 6-8 for publishing. This in turn has improved the quality of the writing, with some children spending several days on the one piece.'

Ann Crumpton exclaims, 'Oh, for a full-time typist! Many of my 6-7 year olds come from homes where English isn't the mother tongue. So finding someone to help with the mounds of writing is very difficult. Without access to a typewriter let alone the typing skills, I started publishing the children's work in my own hand. The workload became impossible and I was worried about the children who had little English, so we began writing for two purposes. The first kind, associated with class themes, was sometimes done in groups and was generally part of Social Studies, Science or a Language theme. It greatly benefited the children with poor English skills. Usually brief, it was handwritten by them or me and displayed around the room with craft work to illustrate it. Everyone had some of this "published". The second kind, free choice writing, gave

Ten year old Kerrie tests her friends with riddles from a classmate's Joke Book.

A proud author, 12 year old Karen has completed the illustrations of her published book which she shares eagerly with a friend.

children competent in English the chance to write involved stories while I assisted the others. We shared much of this writing but it was the child's decision whether to publish or not. In this way the needs of all the children seem to be catered for.'

Bob Spencer is part of the growing band of teachers who find they must call on the services of parents when school personnel can no longer handle the volume of writing: 'Interested mothers volunteered their service as typists for us. They became our "printery". The children and the teachers prepare the writing so it can be easily read by the typists. Any specific instructions for layout, spacing, etc., are added by the child. A "Publishing Folder" is sent along daily to a central place where our "printery" works, though some mothers collect the writing each day, preferring to type at home. They enjoy being involved and express great interest in the quality of the children's work.' He is thrilled by the 'communications network' that has evolved, and agrees with John Brownlow that, 'The parents can clearly see the benefits of the approach in the quality of the writing.'

Publication Other Than by a 'Book'. The problem of finding and retaining the services of good typists has led teachers and children to look for other forms of publication supplementary to 'books':
- keeping a journal or diary;
- reading the story onto tape, with some sound effects;
- making slide-sound sets in association with craft and photography;
- making posters, cards, displays, advertisements;
- writing letters to each other, to another class or school, etc.;
- drama-writing and acting out plays (or puppet shows);
- readers' theatre — spoken presentation of a script without acting.

A Class Publications Committee. Jo Parry declares children need to learn how to publish just as much as they need to learn how to write. To this end the children in her senior primary class form Publication Committees. When the author has completed a piece of writing he or she

Ten year old Christopher, having drafted his cartoon sequence, now draws carefully for the published book.

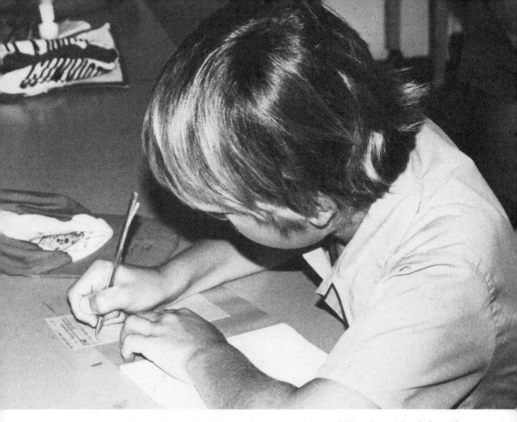

Nine year old Daniel fills in the borrower's card, to take a child-authored book from the library.

chooses several class members to help in the publication cycle of the writing. Together they decide the mode, format, layout, and medium (paint, crayon, etc.) which will best suit the given piece. Armed with all sorts of cardboard and paper, scissors, pens, glue, etc., they begin to plan the work. Black cardboard with silver lettering was chosen for a story about ghosts. A collage effect was used for another. Photographs of plasticine models illustrated another. With the help of the craft teacher these children have produced unique and stimulating books. The children continually peruse commercial picture books for new ideas. Whilst the author always has the final say, everyone does something to help publish the book. The script of the story is sometimes typed in, or written in with various colours and pens by the children and/or the teacher. Publication has taken on a new meaning in this class.

Classroom Borrowing System. Many classes have actually begun their own 'borrowing system', as Barbara McNamara explains: 'The children wanted to take home their own and their classmates' books. In order to keep track of the books we began a card system for borrowing. Each child has a card (18cm x 14cm) with his or her name across the top. It is divided into four columns: Name of Author; Title; Date Borrowed; Date Returned. The children fill in their cards on coming into the room before class, for both returning and borrowing. We store the cards in a cut-down, covered washing powder carton. The children love this system. They enjoy reading each other's writing and feel quietly proud about others reading their books. It is a useful record for me, as I can see at a glance the amount they are reading. I'm quite sure the quality of writing and illustrations have improved since we began this system.'

A 5 Year Old's Idea of Revising for Publication

'I'm writing a book of jokes,' said 5 year old Graham as I sat down beside him. 'Want to hear them?'

He began reading: 'How do you make a dog bark? You get . . .' He stopped.

'I think you've left out a word there,' I suggested. 'Why don't you read it through again and touch the words on your page as you read them, so you can find what you've left out.'

Graham began to read again, touching his words. '*You*, I've left out *you*.' Picking up his orange pencil he wrote *y* in the appropriate place.

Moving on to the next joke he stopped at the place where he had left out *he*, picked up his pencil again and began to write. The letters didn't seem to make sense to me so I asked, 'What have you written?'

'Oh, it's a message for my teacher. It says, "I did leave out some words." She'll know now and if she can't read it, she will come and ask me. Then she can publish it.'

I was left speechless.

Translated, Graham's *Joke Book* reads:

How do you make a dog bark? You (added) get some matches
h   d   y   mak   u do Buk y   gt   mas

and you get a barrel of oil. It goes WOOF.
Ed y   gt u Bl   o oy i g   wofu

What did pink panther do when he trod on an ant? Because it
w   pi b   p   d w   t   o u Ent B k o s i

goes 'Dead-ant, dead-ant.'
gos d   et   d   et

The message Graham wrote during editing for his teacher reads:

I did leave out some words.
I bb l   otu s   ws

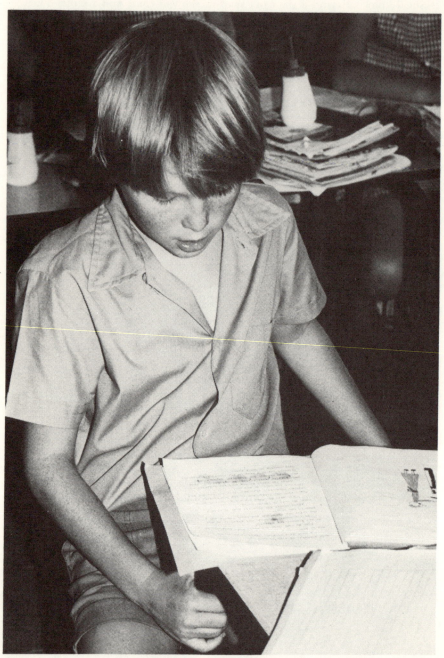

Ten year old Bradley enjoys reading his peers' writing.

CHAPTER 6

Writing and the Curriculum

A surprise feature of the process-conference approach is the change it is bringing to learning in all aspects of the daily curriculum. *Writing IS central to school learning* and teachers are continually amazed at its 'by-product effects' in their classrooms. Sue Smith, for example, says . . .

● 'The writing session is more than learning about writing. It is also a socialising, a counselling, and a sharing time. We teachers so often put pressure on children in learning situations that they fear to admit their faults or express their feelings—but not so in writing! During the writing time I've drawn very close to my children. We share joys and concerns about their writing and themselves and this carries them over into the rest of the day. We've become a large family with . . . a strong respect for each other.'

Writing Helps Reading. Writing and reading are the two sides of the literacy coin—inseparable! And they should be inseparable in the school curriculum. Teachers have long accepted that reading helps in developing children's writing but only now, through this conference approach, are they realising how much their children's reading development can be helped by writing. Not only the teachers see this; it can often be realised by older children who are new to the approach. Here are a few of the replies of Year 6 children at Narwee Public School to the question: *'Has this writing program helped your reading?'*

• 'Since we have been doing this writing I have become more interested in books. Before, I read only what we had to read at school but now my brother recommends books to me and so does my Mum.'
• 'Conference writing has helped me in reading because now I put more expression into my reading. When people are talking I change my voice and when there are commas I let you hear there are commas.'
• 'I am reading different types of books. I read stories other kids write and I like them, so it puts me onto books like what they write.'
• 'I go to the library more to get books out on what I'm writing about. So I am reading lots more.'

Reading and Writing Can Merge. Colleen Larkin, Chris Cookman and Louise Murray explain that they don't *teach* reading—at least, not as they used to . . .

● 'When we began the process writing we decided to use the morning period when the children were fresh and full of enthusiasm. If you walked into our rooms during writing you would find a relaxed and informal atmosphere with children sitting in various places in the room, all at different stages of the writing process.

'Reading was *taught* at a different time of the day. Like many teachers we believed we should teach it in a very structured way, taking our children carefully through a set of given readers with various games and activities in order to teach the necessary words in the prescribed reader.

'But things have changed. During the year, reading and writing began to merge into one happy, pressure-free and stimulating session. The non-readers in the class who used to approach the reading lesson with trepidation have gained confidence and now *want* to read because they know it isn't a crime to make mistakes. Through writing the children have come to believe that all genuine efforts in reading and writing are acceptable. Invented spelling strategies are being applied *to their reading*; as a result the word attack skills we previously so carefully identified and "taught" are being learnt naturally as the children need them. Similarly, they are learning such "phonics" as they need and are not only able to "sound out" words better but also will attempt an educated guess at unknown words in the context of a story.

'Of course we still, in a sense, do teach reading. How? We let the children READ. The introductory flashcard drill and written comprehension exercises have been cut to a minimum; in fact, they are used only with the few children who seem to need them. The reading materials come from various sources—the library, the children's own writing, and many reading schemes—instead of being confined to one scheme. Just as children can choose their own topic in writing they now choose their own reading material too. They set their own goals and

Kindergarten children enjoy reading each other's published books and talking about them.

expectations in learning and to our constant amazement reach higher levels of success than we'd ever set for them. All our children now read confidently at their own level and pace without feelings of inadequacy arising from "I am only at Level 2 whereas my friend is reading at Level 4".

'We have truly individualised the learning of reading and writing and now, together with the children, enjoy our "Language Sessions".'

Integrated Language. Kerry Ball tells how her new writing program has led to an integration of the whole language program . . .

● 'I was using the Mt. Gravatt Reading Scheme with my predominantly E.S.L. 5-6 year olds. Our program seemed already too full to add anything else but I agreed to try. To my amazement it was easy. The writing complemented the reading, becoming such a natural component that I wondered how we ever got on without it. The use of language themes and structures in the Mt. Gravatt program was very supportive for the children with limited English. Drama also played a large part in our language program, involving movement, facial expressions, mime, role play, etc.

'Through the drama, reading and writing we have now integrated our language work. It all seems so natural. Children spend a large part of each day talking about, acting out and writing on various themes and topics. Reading follows naturally.'

Writing Can Foster Peer-tutoring. Even young children can help each other, as Margaret Newton found . . .

● 'I've become increasingly aware of how strong and valuable peer group influence can be. When 4 and 5 year olds begin to take part in the writing periods, they very quickly develop a habit of consulting one another. They are amazingly eager to offer solutions and advice on all sorts of questions. What's more surprising to sceptical adults is that almost invariably such advice is what you would have suggested yourself, if you weren't so strongly committed to leaving control of the learning in the child's hands. Even more disconcerting in one way, and thrilling in another, is the realisation that sometimes it's the sort of advice you'd have loved to give — if only you'd thought of it first!'

Writing Can Break Down 'Breakthrough' Barriers. The widely used reading aid, 'Breakthrough to Literacy', often produces over-reliance on its cardboard words so that children form a habit of writing stilted sentences. How can the process-conference approach overcome this habit? Anne McNamara suggests ways to 'break down the Breakthrough barriers' . . .

● '1. Establish a classroom climate in which initiative and intelligent guesses are accepted, even encouraged.

2. When a child is writing stilted sentences (e.g. I see mum.) write a question underneath (e.g. What is mum doing?), then help the child to write the answer — the child will enjoy what can become a written conversation with the teacher perhaps extending over several days.

3. Praise the child's every effort, particularly when the writing begins to move away from the stilted sentences — and be sure other children hear the praise.

4. Allow the children time to read each other's writing both in draft and published form. It gives them ideas for their own.

5. When reading stories to the class, sometimes choose one for the children to retell, act out and rewrite as a group on large sheets of paper. This provides a model for them to follow.

6. Set up a letter-writing system in which the children write to the teacher or a sympathetic adult who will reply to them. This can be extended to writing to each other.

7. Encourage children to keep a diary for special days or outings. They can use drawings and invented spelling to record their experiences.'

Writing Can Help the E.S.L. Child. A whole book needs to be written on the manifold ways in which process-conference writing can help second language learners. Wendy Stewart provides one vivid example . . .

● 'Seven year old Alex, Chilean-born, entered my class after only two months in Australia. He could speak, read and write in Spanish but had practically no English. His first attempt at story "writing" was to draw elaborate pictures and try to tell me about them in his limited English. This went on for several weeks until one day be began to write a short simple sentence, inventing his spelling with a Spanish accent.

'Confidence grew daily as he experimented with English words and spellings. Stories increased in length and complexity. When he was unsure of the word he needed in English he would refer to another Spanish-speaking child for a translation. But suddenly after ten weeks, he stopped. I was most concerned. The only reason he gave for his reluctance to write was, "I don't know what to write". He seemed to have reached a level of frustration where his ideas for stories had outstripped his ability to use English. During this period I let him draw and talk to me, encouraging his friend to translate for him where necessary. He listened to work other children wrote, including that of Year 4 children who came regularly to our class to share their writing with us. Alex was listening and talking but still not writing.

'Suddenly he began again—this time writing imaginary pieces rather than true life experiences. Now, after six months writing, he is composing confidently, attempting English structures and words that are new to him. (Still with a Spanish accent!) His progress in writing has been most helpful to me, indicating clearly the language structures where he most needs help. Our conference sessions have been a time of teaching these structures at the point of need, with evident improvement in his learning of English.'

Writing Can Produce Responsibility in Learning. Shirley Stokes credits writing with breeding a new sense of responsibility and independence among her young learners . . .

● 'In the early stages of our new writing program I found that children were finishing their work at different times. How could I prevent the noise and silliness of the idle? We discussed possible activities and wrote them up on a chart. From time to time the activities changed (they were generally of the Maths and Reading kind). I allowed free choice, but if any silliness

Twelve year old Saha has written in English a folk story told to her in Arabic by her Lebanese grandmother and so has made it available to the whole class.

took place the child had to put away the activity and do something I'd set (never as interesting!).

'They soon began to select carefully, with a commitment to the work because it was their choice. They became more responsible in their work, often discussing possible answers and seeking advice from one another. This ability to work more independently occurred in all areas of the curriculum. I began to use the conference in Maths and Reading with as much success as in writing. The positive classroom atmosphere that has resulted is far more conducive than was the old order to their learning and my sanity!'

While immersed in the detail of observation Marilyn Rigg finds that a checklist of 'things to watch' is useful.

CHAPTER 7

Response and Evaluation[1]

CONTENTS

Evaluation is in essence a helpful response to a child's efforts;
    it can also draw the child into useful self-evaluation.
Evaluation needs to 'value' all stages of the writing process;
    it shouldn't be limited to the end part, the finished product.
Evaluation can be kept simple and not become time-consuming;
    it can chiefly be part of each day's classroom activities.

These considerations guide the evaluation of writing in process-conference classrooms. The teachers, moment by moment, feel themselves to be fully involved in *assessing* children's handling of all stages of the writing process.

'Assessing' is the appropriate word for most of what they do; 'to assess', in an original meaning, was 'to sit beside and assist or advise' (L.) — which perfectly symbolises the individualised 'conference', with teacher and young writer conferring together. And periodically the teacher reviews the assessment observations in order to make a thoughtful *evaluation*, a general estimate of the writer's progress, the better to help the child, or inform the parents, or meet the school's policy on records.

This chapter is not only for teachers who are settling into the new approach but also for principals who find a 'mix' of traditional and new writing teachers on their staff and realise that only new forms of evaluation will do justice to the new approach. In what follows they will find that 'process evaluation', while not time-consuming, is far more rigorous, more well-informed, more helpful to the child than traditional 'marking' or 'grading' of a 'composition' written at a single sitting.

1. The Teacher's Initial Evaluation of the Writing Program

Evaluation has an overlooked side. While its obvious side is its attempt to estimate a child's progress, its overlooked side is what that estimate *implies* about the effectiveness of the teacher's program.

Logically, then, the first step in evaluation ought to be taken before the class arrives, at the beginning of the year: the teacher needs to review the effectiveness of his or her last year's program.

---

[1] This chapter contributed by R. D. Walshe.

When such a self-evaluation has been made, the teacher will probably want to set down an outline of the improved program for the coming year. Here is an example, with main points listed under 'four essential concerns':

WRITING PROGRAM: PRIORITIES

'The children's progress depends largely on the context-for-writing that this program provides. My general aim is a "writing workshop" atmosphere. [In this classroom, reading too is strongly promoted, no less than writing. —R.D.W.]

'(1) I will continually promote the importance of writing —
• will point to its importance in learning and adult life;
• provide plenty of time to write;
• show that it helps handwriting, spelling, language, reading;
• read aloud daily to convey 'the sound of writing';
• build up the spirit of a 'writing workshop';
• myself write with the class at least once a week.

'(2) I will secure an abundance and range of writing —
• will basically encourage free-choice, personal-experience topics,
      but also writing on classroom 'situations', e.g. improvisations;
• allow a degree of choice in subject-area writing;
• encourage, but not impose, writing about literature;
• demonstrate ways to think-up, ask for, and research ideas.

'(3) I will focus on experiencing writing as a 'process' —
• will continually explain 'process' — a steady clarifying of ideas;
• foster everyday discussion of writing in 'process' terms,
      e.g. pre-writing, first draft, revision/editing, publishing;
• notice whenever possible 'writing models' in literature,
      and use children's published work as models;
• steadily attend to technical problems at the point of need,
      e.g. spelling, punctuation, grammar, structure.

'(4) I will provide real readers for the children's writing —
• will respond myself to their writing at its 'process' stages;
• do this chiefly through my 'conferences' with them;
• also promote 'writing partners' and 'peer conferences';
• publish child's choice (fully revised) of one in 4-5 pieces;
• as well as classroom readers, sometimes find outside readers;
• applaud and feature good writing whenever it appears;
• keep asking, 'What will readers expect of your writing?'

'In this start-of-year context established by my program, the class will begin to write, and my focus will shift from the program to each child's writing. *Then I will turn to the day-by-day building up of my individualised evaluation records which, as I review them periodically throughout the year, will assist me in determining how to help each child. This is in fact the continuing refinement of my program, for each evaluation becomes an individualised program for a child . . . Evaluation and program at this point become one.'*

2. A Choice of Evaluation Records

The teacher, bent on keeping helpful records which are not time-consuming, makes a selection from these:

(a) *'In the Head.'* This may not be acceptable as a *record*, but it has to be mentioned first because regular conferencing with the pupils gives teachers an insight into the child-as-learner which cannot be bettered by any other teaching approach. The teacher sees every child individually at least once a week, apart from briefer opportunities offered by 'Writing Time' to keep in touch with both the child and his or her work. Some teachers argue that they need no more than this direct contact — they have all the evaluation data they need 'in the head'. Why keep other records?

(b) *Anecdotal Record (Observation Record/Diary).* Most teachers, however, acknowledge the value of some kind of 'anecdotal record'; for example, a book in which two pages are given to each child, a page-opening on which observations are scribbled and can be swiftly reviewed when needed. Always to hand on the teacher's table, the book carries comments like, 'Having trouble starting', or 'Begins strongly but trails off', or 'No idea of paragraphs', or 'Success with a poem — is pleased!' By the end of a term such jottings can reveal a pattern of the child's development. They can be used in writing up comments which report the child's progress for the term. They can also help the teacher to decide on a holistic mark or grade if school policy requires one. In particular, a good anecdotal record becomes an individualised *program* which charts strengths and weaknesses and suggests a direction in which the child might move.

(c) *Checklists.* Most teachers feel a need, from time to time, to devise specific checklists, e.g. on currently emphasised punctuation skills or 'Things to Watch When Editing'. A checklist serves to focus attention on present weaknesses or recently demonstrated how-to. It is usually discarded after a short time as the need for it passes.

(d) *The Writing Folder.* The child's writing goes into the Folder and all of it is dated, whether it is a draft, a revision, or a rewritten piece. As the complete record of the child's writing performance the Folder is obviously the most significant evaluation resource. It is also the simplest, least time-consuming record the teacher can keep. It invites a critical eye to make inferences about progress: 'See, if you compare August's writing with that of February, you realise that . . .'. Some teachers, working to a schedule of, say, five conferences a day (apart from unscheduled ones) prepare by making a swift before-school or after-school check on the Folders of the five pupils.

Moreover the four sides of the Folder-as-cover can carry additional information to assist evaluation of the child's involvement with writing, ideas and literary models. That is, the covers carry lists such as 'Topics I Have Written About', 'Topics I May Write About', 'Writing Skills I Have Learned', and 'Books I Have Read This Year' (including ones by class-mates).

(e) *Work Samples.* Some teachers periodically extract samples from the Writing Folder — say, the child's best piece of finished writing for a 4, 5 or 6 weeks period, usually accompanied by its earlier drafts.

(f) *'Published' Books.* A 'work sample' of a special kind is the published writing of the child. The most popular form is the small 'book', either typed or carefully handwritten, with decorated cover. It usually forms part of the class library. Each child can point with pride to a growing number of such well-crafted books. They are evidence that the child has success-fully experienced the full 'process of writing'. Indeed, they are a striving after excellence at the child's level.

(g) *Class Anthologies.* Some teachers require every pupil to select his or her best piece of writing over a month and submit it to the class anthology. Polished, neatly rewritten and often illustrated, this writing is bound into an attractive folder to become a valued part of the class library. From an evaluation point of view, this is another form of 'work sampling'.

3. Evaluation of 'Process' through Conferences

An observer in a conference classroom, watching the teacher work beside one child after another, is usually impressed by this individualising of learning. The observer concludes that it is a superior way of helping the children with their particular writing problems. True enough. But the observer may not realise that simultaneously the teacher is assessing each child's growth as a writer, gathering data for evaluation judgments that will help the writer to advance in ways that go beyond the specific problems of the current piece. Meanwhile the observer notices that much of the teacher's 'conferencing' takes the form of asking questions. This serves to gently push the child towards questioning of his or her own writing process — towards intelligent self-evaluation.

(a) *At the Pre-writing Stage.* The teacher may help the child, chiefly through questions, to find a manageable subject, a point-of-view, and a structure, and may even help with 'getting started'. Good questions are usually the brief, simple kind such as:

• 'What do you think you'll write about?'
• 'Why have you chosen this ahead of other possible topics?'
• 'Do you feel you have enough information to begin writing?'
• 'At which point in the events might you begin the piece?'
• 'Do you think it will interest your readers?'

(b) *At the First Draft Stage.* The 'old model' of writing teaching gave children the impression that the first draft was final. No wonder so many thought they were failures as writers! Now the teacher says encouragingly, 'Anyone can work on a draft to turn it into good writing.' This stage of the writing is assessed *as a draft only*, an initial attempt to get ideas into shape. Attention to correctness of spelling and other surface features is left to the later revision stage. The teacher asks questions arising from an 'empathetic reading', that is, from *within* the meaning-feeling-intention of the writer, rather than from the external viewpoint of an editor or literary critic:

• 'How did it go? Are you pleased with the way it's shaping?'
• 'How can I help you with this piece?'
• 'I think I get your key idea. What would you say it is?'

- 'Do you think you've started right into the subject?'
- 'Which part are you happiest with? . . . not happy with?'
- 'Do you think it might help to explain . . . ?'

(c) *At the 'Revised' Stage.* Here the teacher wants to assess the writer's grasp of revision possibilities — whether many revision options have been considered. Possible questions:
- 'How successfully do you think you've revised?' (The answer to this request for a self-assessment will guide the teacher's further questions.)
- 'Is your title now right?' (*or* your beginning, ending, etc.)
- 'Why did you change that?' (a specific point)
- 'Is anything still nagging — not quite right?'
- 'Will you do another draft?' *or* '. . . let it rest till fresh ideas come?'
- 'Should it be published?' 'In what form?'

4. When School Policy Requires an Evaluation

Traditional and new approaches to teaching writing are rubbing shoulders in most schools. The traditional approach has its traditional mode of evaluation; but how will a teacher of the 'process-conference' approach meet the school's call for end-of-term, half-yearly, or yearly evaluations? Here are some suggestions . . .

Preliminary. Make sure the principal is well-informed as to the organisation and operation of your 'writing classroom', its individualisation of learning, its methodical improvement of writing through a process of drafting and revising, and its admirable published results. Invite the principal to come to your room, to conduct some conferences with pupils, and to look at examples of how their writing has improved through draft — revision — publication.

Offer a Well-informed Evaluation. For example, offer the wide-ranging evaluation below. You may also need to suggest that:
- to be fair, evaluation should be based not on a single piece of writing but on the pupil's better writing of the period under review (at the least, on three pieces);
- an evaluation is best expressed in words, since a numerical mark or letter grade is an uncertain quantification of the complex elements in writing. (How can all those 'Features of Writing', above, be summed up in a mark?).

A Wide-ranging and Specific Evaluation:
- you reflect on what you know of the child;
- review the child's published writing;
- review the contents of his or her Writing Folder;
- review the comments in your anecdotal record.

A special conference with the child should be an integral part of this evaluation. The child thereby experiences a review of his or her writing over the given period, with opportunity to reflect and comment on progress and problems. At the end of the session the teacher presents a helpful summing up. Then the teacher writes the evaluation *comments* required by school policy . . . These special conferences do take time, but they happen only two or three times a year and are important for the pupils. The class goes on with writing and reading while they are taking place.

Q: What if school policy demands a grade or mark? A grade or mark won't help the child in the way your thoughtful comments will. It is 'rank-ordering'; in effect, you are being asked to write down the numbers 1-30, or whatever number of pupils you have, and rank them according to your 'guesstimate' — which, mercifully, can be done very quickly! You then allocate the grades or marks down the list, simply by subjective decision, since there can be no 'objective standards' for this traditional practice.

Q: What if school policy wants a grade or mark or comment based on only one piece of writing? You might propose this course: that you will ask each child to (a) choose his or her best piece from the Writing Folder, (b) review the piece, polish it further, rewrite and proofread it, then (c) submit it for assessment.

Q: What if the school will not depart from the traditional procedure, namely, 'a composition written in exam conditions to a set time-limit'? You must point out that these are special (not to say artificial) conditions for writing and they are alien to your children's experience. Ask that concessions be made to what 'process' writers are used to; for example, (a) allow topic choice by the child or at least notification of a topic (or choice from several) a day previously, to allow for some preparation; (b) allow the right to return to the test-draft the following day and revise and rewrite it. If this is not conceded, you have no alternative but to spend time *teaching your class to do the test*, because this test demands a specific form of writing ('one-shot drafting') and therefore needs specific practice.

Q: What criteria should govern the evaluation of a single sample of writing (or more than one) carried out in test conditions? You are not being permitted to evaluate what is most important, namely, the child's *process* of writing. You must judge something very limited, namely, the test *product*. School conditions won't allow you time for a scrupulous 'analytical scoring' of all those 'features of writing' discussed above, so you must find a practicable alternative in what is increasingly called 'holistic marking' — a term which gratuitously suggests that the *whole* composition, everything, is looked at. In fact this method is descended from traditional 'general impression marking'. Honest markers admit they can't think 'holistically' of everything; they can only try to keep a limited range of 'features' or 'criteria' in mind. So, first, think out a list of criteria before you begin marking; for example, Points 6-15 in 'Things to Watch' of Robert Hughes (p. 68), or fewer, or more. Second, swiftly review the papers to locate 'guide samples' (or 'range-finders') which exemplify 'competency levels' from high to low. Third, read all the papers and allocate each to one of the levels. Finally, allot the numerical mark or letter grade, with or without accompanying comment, as required by school policy.

5. The Teacher's Perception of 'Good Writing'

At all stages the teacher is looking for *quality* in the child's writing. But what is good writing? This question has been answered in hundreds of ways, testifying to the complexity of writing but never arriving at an agreed answer.[2]

So every teacher must individually decide what good writing is, and relate this perception to each child's performance. Obviously evaluation will be the more effective if the teacher has thought this matter through. It will be even more effective if the teacher sometimes writes along with the children, and makes the question, 'What is good writing?' an issue of daily classroom discussion.

Here is a concise but comprehensive view of the *features of writing*, adapted from P.E.T.A.'s *Teaching Literature*, 1983, p. 116. It is offered as a checklist from which a teacher may select elements felt to be worth watching in current writing or evaluating.

FEATURES OF WRITING

(a) *First Impressions*
A first reading of the piece provides important 'first impressions':
Good title? Easy to 'get into'? Is its early interest sustained?
Does the writer's 'voice' come through? (personality/flavour)
Will intended readers, in a normal reading, 'get the message'? (effect)

(b) *Information* ('meaning')
A second, detailed reading assesses message/content/meaning:
Is there enough to satisfy intended readers? (data and explanation)
Is it specific, descriptive, curiosity-satisfying, . . .?
Might cuts be made to improve conciseness?

(c) *Organisation* ('structure')
Detailed reading looks for underlying pattern or plan:
Is there a well-sequenced development of ideas?
A good 'lead' (opening)? An effective ending?
Will readers get an impression of order, unity? (coherence/logic)

(d) *Language Choices* ('surface')
Detailed reading checks surface features:
Wording: wide vocabulary, used aptly, economically? correct spelling?
Sentences: lively, varied, well-linked, punctuated, correct?
Paragraphs: well developed, not tediously long, smoothly linked?

N.B. The abstract term 'style' has not been used. Whatever it means will come out—as far as verbalisation is possible—in answering the specific questions.

---

2 P.E.T.A. President, Barry Dwyer, comments: 'Asked what good writing is, many parents and even some teachers think at once of mechanical correctness, but that of course is secondary to *meaning* and all the factors in writing that go into achieving it. I like to quote Donald Murray, who says emphatically, "Good writing is what makes the reader feel or think, and the best writing is what makes the reader feel *and* think".'

6. Deciding What to Watch (or Report)

The teacher, moving from child to child around the class, is observing hundreds of specific *aspects of the writing process* and hundreds of specific *features of writing*. Only a relatively small number of these observations will be jotted down in the teacher's records. Even more generally the teacher may need to draw out a short list of 'Things to Watch' in the children's writing performance, whether for day-by-day checking purposes or to report to the principal or parents.

Such a list must be compiled individually by the teacher, growing out of his or her perception of good writing, effective process, and the current needs of the class.

Here is an example of a 'minimum list' currently being used by Robert Hughes of Loftus Public School for his Year 4 class. Point 1 is attitudinal, points 2-5 cover process issues, points 6-15 features of writing.

	Above Average	Satisfactory	Experiencing Difficulties	Comments:
1. A willing attitude to writing?				
2. Able to select own topics?				
3. Able to gather information?				
4. Able to write a first draft fluently?				
5. Able to revise and rewrite?				
6. Presents enough information?				
7. Achieves clarity of expressions?				
8. Sequences ideas logically?				
9. Writes openings that arouse interest?				
10. Writes satisfying or dramatic endings?				
11. Reveals a growing vocabulary?				
12. Structures sentences correctly?				
13. Is getting the idea of paragraphing?				
14. Shows improving control of mechanics?				
15. Shows improving control of spelling?				

To emphasise how specific such a list has to be for a given teacher and class, here is a very different list which Marilyn Rigg uses with her kindergarten class at Sylvania Heights Public School. It pays even stronger attention to 'process' issues:

1. Shows enthusiasm for writing?
2. Knows where to sit, and with whom?
3. Readily selects writing materials, and starts?

4. Can find topics to write about?
5. Uses drawing and/or talk to focus thought?
6. Willingly 'invents' spellings, even of 1-2 letters?
7. Reads back carefully before writing next word?
8. Has grasped left-to-right and top-down directions?
9. Is spacing between words?
10. Is beginning to use some punctuation?
11. Shows signs of imaginative thought/storying?
12. In reading aloud, speaks only the words written?

7. Ways to Keep Parents Informed

When the conference approach to writing is first launched, parents need to be informed. This calls for an explanatory letter, perhaps backed by a 'parent evening'. At this or a later meeting, some schools invite the parents to take up a pen themselves and go through the main stages of 'process' writing. They find this intriguing. Then their cooperation is enlisted in encouraging their child to report to them on school writing exploits and sometimes carry out some writing of the pleasurable kind in the home.

Schools use a variety of ways to keep parents informed:
• Send home a periodical report on the child's writing.
• In a regular class newsletter, give prominence to writing.
• At mid-term and end-of-term, send home, say, a 'Progress Book' or 'Writing Evaluation Folder', containing:
  examples of writing done at beginning and end of the period;
  or the child's choice of 'My Best Piece(s) of Writing';
  or all the child's writing in all subjects for one week;
  or a published 'book', with draft and revisions attached;
  or a report by the child on 'Our Writing Time', plus samples.
• The children can write to their parents every term telling what they have been doing in writing and listing new things they have learned — one more real piece of writing!
• When writing is typed for publication, a carbon copy or photocopy can be made so that two books result, the original for the class library, the copy for the child to take home.
• Parents can be invited to visit during 'Writing Time'.
• Every opportunity can be taken to display the children's best writing on parent nights and special occasions such as Book Week.

Schools Taking Part in the
St. George Writing Project K-12

Engadine West Public School
Kurnell Public School
Sylvania Heights Public School
Oatley West Public School
Narwee Public School
Campsie Public School
Hampden Park Public School
Ramsgate Public School
Hurstville South Public School
St. Aloysius School, Cronulla

Teachers Who Have Contributed

Engadine West, N.S.W.
John Brownlow
Julie Flavell
Chris Cookman
Colleen Larkin
Louise Murray

Kurnell, N.S.W.
Barbara McNamara
Sue Hewitt
Francis Kean

Sylvania Heights, N.S.W.
Jill Sweeting
Tom McCabe
Christine Green
Marilyn Rigg

Oatley West, N.S.W.
Marilyn Kelly
Judy Wagner

Narwee, N.S.W.
Denise Stuckey

Campsie, N.S.W.
Wendy Stewart
Ann Crumpton
Shirley Stokes
Kerry Ball

Ramsgate, N.S.W.
Joan Hoyle
Bob Spencer
Prod Foulkare

St. Aloysius, Cronulla, N.S.W.
Dot Gamble
Sr. Margaret Harrison
Sue Hutchins
Cath Croucher
Sue Smith

Grays Point, N.S.W.
Robyn Platt

Hurstville South, N.S.W.
Margaret Newton

Reservoir East, Vic.
Jo Parry

Duffy Primary School, A.C.T.
Anne McNamara

Loftus, N.S.W.
Robert Hughes

Curtin Primary School, A.C.T.
Dorothy Jauncey

Denise Ryan
Language Consultant, Metropolitan
West Region, N.S.W. Dept. of
Education

Index